Drifted
back in time

Mill 4/7/08

MILLIE L. McGHEE

Drifted back in time

DEEP SECRETS REVEALED

TATE PUBLISHING *& Enterprises*

Published by Tate Publishing & Enterprises, LLC
127 E. Trade Center Terrace | Mustang, Oklahoma 73064 USA
1.888.361.9473 | www.tatepublishing.com

Tate Publishing is committed to excellence in the publishing industry. The company reflects the philosophy established by the founders, based on Psalm 68:11,
"The Lord gave the word and great was the company of those who published it."

Book design copyright © 2007 by Tate Publishing, LLC. All rights reserved.
Cover design by Kellie Southerland
Interior design by Janae J. Glass

Published in the United States of America

ISBN: 978-1-60462-244-7
1. History: United States: 19th Century   2. Fiction: Romance: Historical

07.10.31

"There is something addicting about a secret."
J. Edgar Hoover (1895–1972)

To my granddaughter, Tyara Reed, for her support and love for my work.

To my husband, Dr. Leslie L. Morris, for helping me face up to my fears of those bad spirits that lived inside of my heart. He also helped me feel strong, and ready to move forward with my life.

Finally, in loving memory of all my ancestors, special thoughts to my Big Daddy, Clarence Allen.

ACKNOWLEDGEMENTS

I am so thankful for the Afro-American Historical and Genealogical Society, Inc. for supporting me during the time I needed them the most. Specifically, the AAHGS—Arkansas; AAHGS—Central California; AAHGS—James Dent Walker; AAHGS—Patricia Liddell Researchers; AAHGS—New Jersey; AAHGS —North Carolina/Piedmont-Triad; AAHGS—African American Genealogy Group of Charlottesville/Albemarle County, Virginia, and the AAHGS—Huntsville, AL,.

Special thanks to Mr. Lucius Bowser, the late Mr. Julian Burke, and Mr. George Ott—all historians and genealogists.

I want to thank FBI agent M. Wesley Swearingen for encouraging me to complete my research and be proud of my work.

Thanks to my lovely parents, William and Alberta McGhee for being supportive in every way possible.

Lots of love to my wonderful and loving children, Kymberly and Vincent Reed.

Thanks to all my nieces and nephews and cousins all over the US for loving me.

Cherie C. Stewart, my best friend who was so supportive of me. I miss her.

Many thanks to the following people who were always supportive and caring during a very hard time in my life: my sisters—Queen, Lydia, Sylvia, and Jeannette; my brothers—Douglas, Bobby—and to all those who call me sister. My godchildren: Danny, Aaron, Chip, Yuena, Larry, Azie, and Skylar.

More to thank: Kristy Hoover Sullivan, Haley Sullivan, Danny Arguello, Jacqueline Groves, Denise Boulden, Mertine Moore, Barbara Reynolds, Aaron Brown, Wallace Allen, Tamela Tenpenny-Lewis, Eugene Dillanado, Nadine Dillanado, Beverly Brown James Cotton, Regina Johnson, Nathan Johnson, and Jacqueline Martin.

Thanks to the mayors of wonderful cities: Mayor J.C. Woods, Mayor Robert Bowser, Mayor Jim Dailey, Mayor William Alexander and the Late Mayor Glenn Cunningham. Judge Jack Jones and Governor Mike Huckabee, many thanks.

FOREWORD

It gives me great pleasure to give this statement to the readers of this wonderful story. A spiritual journey by the author, Millie L. McGhee, *Drifted Back In Time: Deep Secrets Revealed* is a breath of fresh air for me. I think all readers will feel this author's soul as they read this empowering novel of grace and hope for all of us in the future. I knew that there was something powerful about her excitement to find her roots, and was delighted to support her in every way that I could to bring closure to her spirit from her past.

Nobody I know would have picked J. Edgar Hoover as a relative. So, when she found this history from her oral stories told to her by her parents and grandfather, I believed her and wanted to help her through this very deep, dark task into the past.

During her years of many trips and long nights of writing, I knew she was on to a great project, and she was determined to find the truth. When I finally got a chance to review her work, knowing her background of illiteracy after graduating from high school, I was so proud of her accomplishing her goals. The many hours of research and study she put into educating herself was amazing and exciting to watch.

I have had the opportunity to look at hours of video

tapes, TV and radio interviews, and many pictures, as well as the docudrama *What's Done In The Dark*, which she produced. The research was done over a period of ten years. It was great to have had the opportunity to travel with her in 2002 when we traveled back to Mississippi to review the research done there in 2000.

It was very interesting to find this history that was told to her when she was only ten years old. The tombstones of Hoovers and Allens in McComb, MS, were side by side. I learned from her genealogist and other historians that such a practice of having slaves buried close and adjacent to the master's family is an uncommon situation, one seldom seen or discovered in the history of genealogy. Normally the slave owners' cemetery plots are distantly separated from their slaves. This unique arrangement was an important highlight of the trip to the Hoover plantation for the author and all of us.

I had the privilege of reviewing the census records, wills, vital statistics, reports, and news articles with historians—everything that was researched by the author. I found the documents clearly understandable in the connection to her newfound white cousin. Conspicuously, however, there were no accurate documented records showing how J. Edgar Hoover related to the white Hoovers, but clear record to the Black Allens.

I found this work educational and inspiring; I hope it will encourage many others to find it in their heart to learn to forgive and love all people, as it will help America heal its wounds.

Dr. Leslie L. Morris, MD
Psychiatrist

PREFACE

This story is a fictional account of a young woman whose life was influenced by stories she had been told as a young girl growing up in Mississippi. The work is also influenced by actual research into family genealogy she discovered as she tried to understand feelings she had all of her life. The story is uniquely told in the form of flashbacks and memories that came to her as she began to put the story on paper.

The story was revealed to her in dreams, often in the form of visits by the author to the past. As she wrote and as the stories evolved, they took on a life of their own. They became vivid accounts as if she were actually there. The unique telling of this story and her memories of this time in history may seem different than other historical accounts.

Many people have written of the persecution of slaves by their masters and the inhumane treatment many received. This story indicates a different kind of relationship between the master and the slave. Keep in mind that this is one women's memory and interpretation of a story told to her over the years. It is written in the dialect of the times and the depictions of the relationships are influenced by the oral history passed from her grandfather and mother.

Subsequent discoveries depicted in other works have given evidence to these unique relationships. For example, in her research slaves were found buried in the same graveyards as the master family. This was an occurrence that was not generally found in the days of slavery and post Civil War America.

Many people have asked me to write my true-life story coming from Mississippi to Los Angeles, California. I hope it will inspire many other young people to find their roots and hopefully write about it as I did. It has been a tedious journey finding my roots and learning so much more about my family. I will cherish the ten years that I spent getting in touch with the spirits of my ancestors. Doing this work helped me get to know myself better and change what I could in my life, as well as accept the things that I couldn't change. I am able to move forward and help those that want to be helped and understand those that wish to remain the same.

—Millie L. McGhee

THE AUTHOR'S ORAL STORY

It was one cold, dreary day in mid April, and I realized I didn't feel happy when the sun wasn't up. Where I lived, people didn't say the sun was shining; they would say, the sun is up.

I was only ten years old in 1957, as happy as any ten-year-old could be, until that one April day I got into an argument in my history class with a classmate about a man nobody in our part of the world liked. We were in the middle of studying the presidents of the United States, when a boy named Lamar said, "J. Edgar Hoover is the president!"

I thought to myself, *Hoover...where have I heard that name?*

In a flash, I remembered. My grandfather "Big Daddy" and my mother had told me stories about my ancestors who were slaves, owned by the Hoover family. History was my favorite subject, and I knew J. Edgar Hoover was in the FBI, and not a president. So I said, "What's wrong with you? That Hoover man is in the FBI and he is not a president. We are studying US presidents, just in case you didn't notice."

The teacher, Mr. Gatlin, was not happy with us fighting in the class, but I could tell he was impressed with my knowledge of what position J. Edgar Hoover held. He listened to our debate for a few moments, then said, "Now students, we must stop this argument and get back on the subject of United State Presidents."

Then I noticed Lamar making faces at me, obviously feeling pleased with himself for getting under my skin. That only made me madder. Besides, it was not intelligent for him to think that way, and not be told the correct history about this Hoover man, and the United States Presidents. The teacher caught him making faces at me.

"Just to be clear on the discussion between the two of you—J. Edgar Hoover is not, and has never been, president of the United States, so let's move on to the subject that we are studying today."

That was fine with me, and I smiled, all justified, at Lamar. He didn't like it at all, and jumped up and said, "Well, he has more power than any president!"

When he said that, it made me angry, because I knew who this man was and wondered if Lamar knew it as well. So I said, "Teacher, I wonder if he knows the difference between an FBI agent, and the President of the United States?"

The teacher realized that I was serious about my history and wanted Lamar to be clear, so he said,

"Lamar, Mr. Hoover is in charge of the FBI, and has nothing to do with the president's job. So, can we move on to our lesson for today?"

This still didn't stop Lamar from believing that J.

Edgar Hoover had greater power, and he said, "He has more power than the president; I can see that myself. He runs this country."

I could tell Lamar was not going to give up, and so could the teacher, but he tried again to help the boy understand that he was on the wrong track. He said, "Lamar, this may be what a lot of people in this country think, but you need to know that J. Edgar Hoover is not running this country, and we are not going to discuss the subject any more today, okay?"

Lamar was not happy about the debate ending, but nodded his head okay to the teacher. I couldn't wait to get to my Big Daddy's house to talk to him about J. Edgar Hoover, because I believed that Big Daddy knew pretty much everything about anything.

When I got home, Mother was in the kitchen cooking dinner, and Father was talking to her about church. I walked in and said, "Mom and Dad, can I ask a question?"

They both stopped talking; they could tell that I had something important to me on my mind, and Mother said, "Yes, Mildred, you may ask."

This made me happy to be able to talk to my mother and father about my history class and I said, "I learned something in my history class today about a man name Hoover, and I want to ask Big Daddy about it. So when can we visit him?"

They just looked at each other and wondered what it was that troubled me so much about this Hoover man. My father asked, "What is it, Mildred? Maybe we can help."

∾

When my father asked I started to get frightened because he was very strict and I thought mean some times. My parents were proud parents of ten children, although only nine of us were living, since my brother, James Edward died of pneumonia at seven months old.

We were all very afraid of my father, because he would get your behind in a minute, and I didn't like getting that belt on my backside. Today it would be called child abuse, the way my father used his belt on us.

Looking back, I believe that he had to do whatever it took to raise that many children without having much of an education himself. Anyway, he didn't kill us, so it was fine. But when he got a certain look in his face, the last thing I'd think of was whether I was doing what he felt needed done. The only thing that I would be thinking was how to keep that belt away from me. And right then, the look on his face meant that I needed to tell him why I wanted to go talk to my grandfather.

So I said, "I had an argument in my history class about a man named Hoover in the FBI. Lamar, one of my classmates, said Hoover was the president, and I told him that he wasn't. I wanted to ask Big Daddy more about our history with the Hoovers that owned Grandmamma Emily."

I could tell that Father was proud of me for wanting to know more about my family roots, and he said, "That is all right, we will take you all to visit this Sunday."

I was so happy, and couldn't wait to go visit my Big Daddy and see his big white house. Sunday finally came, and I was all excited, ready to find out more about my ancestors. We children ran through our small apartment that morning. My father had rules about the girls being fully clothed before leaving their bedroom, so I had to wait for my turn to get into the one bathroom in our place. I often wondered how we all lived in that one-bathroom apartment, and also how we all fit in the car to go visiting and to church, but we did.

When we got to Big Daddy's house, he was sitting, just like always, on the porch with his legs stretched across the banister, smoking his pipe. I jumped out of the car and ran up the stairs to him and sat my small body under his legs. He smiled down at me and said, "Hello little one, what's on you mind today?"

I was so happy and out of breath from running, I couldn't speak for a moment and when I finally could, I said, "Hi, Big Daddy, I love you so much, and I have something I want to talk to you about today, please?"

Now Big Daddy didn't say much, but when he talked, everyone listened. Smiling down at the obviously excited little girl at his feet, he said, "Okay, what is it you want to know today, my child?"

I just jumped right into it. "I was in history class this past week studying the presidents of the United States, and Lamar, that's a boy in my class, said that J. Edgar Hoover was the president, and I told him that was not true."

Big Daddy was looking at me with concern in his face, and said, "You told him right, child."

That made me feel great, and I said, "Big Daddy, Lamar also told the teacher that J. Edgar Hoover had more power than the president, and I was not happy with him saying those things."

Big Daddy had a look on his face that I had never seen before; it was a deep-thought look, and he said, "Well, that could be true, child. Mr. Hoover does have a lot of power. So, little girl what else do you want to know?"

I started to recount to him the oral history stories that were told to me at home, family reunions, and sitting under his legs many times before, when he would say, "Our tradition of storytelling goes all the way back to Africa, where a family member would tell the others the fact of our beginning all the way back to Africa.

"Three very strong women started our family history. The first woman name is unknown. She was called, 'Grandma Elizabeth's Mother.' She was taken from Africa, and impregnated by her slave owner. When the baby was born, it was a girl child and was named Elizabeth Allen.

"Elizabeth also was impregnated by her slave owner with a girl child, and named her Emily Allen, who was my great, great grandmother. Elizabeth Allen passed for white her entire life; she is the second woman to this circle. The third woman is her child Emily Allen, who was left with her father—her slave master—and stepbrothers and sisters. Emily

~

was only nineteen years old when she and her step-brother, Christian Kit Hoover, had a love affair; from that encounter came a child. This child was very special to the family, because he was born on their father's birthday, November 24, 1859, and was Emily's firstborn son. They named this child Ivery Hoover.

"Emily Allen began her survival at that point in her life, making historical history for our family. She had an affair with another white slave owner named Eff McComb. He was a very rich man because the town was named after him or someone in his family. She had a girl child by him, and named her Malinda Allen because she was unmarried to the man. In 1869, old man Christian Hoover [born November 24, 1796] willed Emily to his other son, William Hoover [born 1832], a married man. It wasn't too long before he started getting out of his wife's bed and into bed with Emily.

"Emily had seven children by the Hoover slave owners; we refer to them all as 'Master Hoover.' She was my great, great grandmother. She loved William Hoover; she never left him her whole life. The white wife left and Old Man Hoover and Emily stayed together her entire life—forever."

I sat there thinking, *I may be crossing the line, but I have to know*, so I just blurted it out. "Is J. Edgar Hoover a part of the Hoovers that owned great, great grandmother Emily?"

He didn't answer right away, and slowly took out his pipe, shrugged, and carefully came out with the words, saying, "That old goat is my second cousin."

∼

He paused, then continued, thoughtfully. "Many members of my family were told that our family history was a secret, especially when J. Edgar Hoover was born as Ivery Hoover's outside child. The family was threatened with death to us all if we ever tell that secret. Two people were mysteriously killed— one of them my Uncle Ivery—as an example to all of us—what could happen if any one talked about the deep dark secret going on inside the family."

I began to get real excited, because Mr. Hoover was a very important man, and I had just been told that he was related to us. My heart was jumping out my chest with excitement. Big Daddy knew his little girl, and could tell that I was just itching to let everybody know that I was related to somebody real important.

Then, Big Daddy frowned at me, and I was a little taken back. He didn't look all excited, like I thought he ought to be. No, he was very serious with me, and he said, "Now don't you to go telling anyone that he is related to us. That is a family secret. This man doesn't want to be a part of us."

"Why?" I asked, and went on to say, "I don't understand why we should keep his secret."

Big Daddy's answer was even more serious than before. "Don't you tell anyone! This man doesn't want anyone to know that he is a part of this family."

Big Daddy was starting to frighten me.

"He's passing for white," he said.

Big Daddy was not getting through to me, and he knew it. He looked right into my eyes with that

∽

look that told me he could see clear through to my soul, and said, "If you tell anyone, J. Edgar Hoover will have us all killed as we sleep."

My knees began to shake, but he wasn't done yet.

"We all could be burned to death in our beds," he said.

I was just shocked at what he was saying to me, and asked, "Would he really do that to us, Big Daddy?"

He answered, "Yes, he would, this man doesn't want to be black, and remember he is a powerful man!"

I found myself getting more and more fear in my heart. I believed Big Daddy, of course, and was afraid that if I told anyone, I would kill my entire family, whom I loved so much.

Big Daddy continued, "Now you listen to me child. This man doesn't want to know us, and I want to keep it that way, you hear me?"

He was starting to realize what he had done, and regretted telling me the secret he had kept for so long. In my heart, I was just sorry that my Big Daddy, who I always thought was the strongest man in the world, was so frightened of this man. But I still didn't really understand how such a big thing about such a famous man could be kept secret.

"Wouldn't they ask him about his relatives?" I asked.

Big Daddy looked at me and said, "The law wouldn't find any records showing us related to him. Not anywhere. There won't be any files on that man and us, you can bet on that."

∾

I asked more questions. "Wouldn't they find his birth certificate?"

He looked at me as though he was troubled, and I thought he was angry with me for asking so many questions. But all he wanted was to make sure I understood how important it was that I knew this was a deep dark family secret that was never to be told to anyone.

He continued, "He will destroy all files connecting himself to this family, and I believe he has already done it."

I was too young to understand what was being done to me at that time, and I found myself getting very frightened, until I started shaking badly. Big Daddy noticed and abruptly said, "You go on in the house now."

I knew he wasn't happy about telling me the truth, because our storytelling had never ended that way. All the way home, I was so frightened that I pretended to be asleep in the car so that I wouldn't tell the secret.

When we got home, I jumped out of the car without saying a word to anyone and rushed into the house, trying to get to the restroom first. I felt a heavy burden of responsibility on my shoulders, since it was now my job to keep this dark secret, and to protect my entire family. I didn't dare let my parents question me; I knew I needed to talk to God, right away.

When I reached the privacy of the restroom, I was still terrified, and couldn't understand why my

Big Daddy would frighten me so badly. Then, in my mind I thought, *He wouldn't have done that unless he was trying to protect me.*

I started to pray to God from my heart, begging Him to take that memory away from me. I said, "Please God, don't let me remember this secret in the morning. I am so afraid. I know something important, and I know I'll want to talk to somebody about it. But if I do, my family will be in danger, so I need to lose this memory altogether, I pray you will help me. Amen."

I stayed in my room crying until I fell asleep, hoping I would wake up and the memory would be gone forever. The next morning, I was feeling tired, but the memory was gone, my prayers were answered. I thought to myself, *Well, I was protected by God, it wasn't really gone, just hidden somewhere inside of me where I wouldn't have to look at it and be scared all the time.*

I never spoke of it to anyone, and decided not to ask any more question about ancestors. When they had family reunions, I would pretend I wasn't listening. Every time the kinfolk would get together, they would retell that same old story about great, great grandmamma Emily. She was a slave who had seven babies by the slave master, and one of her children that was given the Hoover surname. Her mother, Elizabeth Allen, who passed for white, came from Africa when she was a child. Nobody knew Elizabeth's mother's name; they were both slaves also.

∾

Those three women were the beginning of our family, and they survived it all. My mother was a wonderful storyteller, and I had always loved listening to her, but I didn't want to hear any more about our ancestors.

With God's help, I'd succeeded in pushing that memory someplace safe in my soul, where I couldn't accidentally blurt something out that would endanger my family.

After growing up to be a teenager, I wanted to become a writer badly, and move far away from Mississippi. I felt that there was nothing left for me there. I knew that if I was going to help my family, I needed to get a good education, and that wasn't likely to happen in that small Mississippi town. We were considered very poor, and that made me very sad. Sad because the other children were mean most of the time, especially those that didn't live in the Projects. I wanted to become closer to God at a very young age, because I knew that there was no meanness in Him, and felt that He would keep me and my family safe from my secret. I joined my father's church, and was baptized in the river at the age of twelve and that was the day, I asked God to come into my soul and live there forever.

I found myself fighting with my brother Bill a lot because of the secrets. I was afraid I might tell him, because I loved him a lot. I often holed in my bedroom in privacy to pray to God for help in my plans to get my family out of the projects and into a good life.

At sixteen, I felt that it was time to learn from

my mother about my birth. Storytelling was great, and one quite day I asked, "Mother, please tells me about the day I was born."

Mother answered, "Well, on November 24, 1947, a little before midnight, you started letting us know you wanted to be born. It was a cold, windy night, and I went into labor with you inside of me kicking and raising habit."

I quickly took a seat on the floor near her feet and said, "Wow! Tell me what happened then, Mother? Did Daddy take you to the hospital?"

Mother looked at me and smiled, and I realized she was feeling happy about me wanting her to tell me this story. She went on, "Well, I went to bed, and no, your father didn't take me to the hospital."

"But Mother, why would you go to bed? Weren't you in pain? When did Daddy take you to the hospital?" I asked.

My mother loved telling stories about how we came into being and how we lived back in the day, and still tells stories today. I am sure that is why I love storytelling, and finding my family roots.

Still laughing at me for being so fired up, Mother said, "Mildred, I know you are excited, and I will finish telling you about your birth, but you must settle down and listen...you were born at home!"

She was right. I was excited to learn the details of my birth, especially after learning that I was born at home. I had many other questions in my mind to ask, but I decided to listen.

∽

My mother was a very pretty woman, with long black hair, high cheekbones, a pointed noise, and nice thick lips—and she stood five feet eleven inches tall. Mother continued, "Well, it was the day before Thanksgiving. I was getting ready for my big family dinner, and you kicked inside my stomach with great determination to be born. I turned to your father and said, 'Honey, this baby is coming. We need to find Miss Leavtcher Seals to deliver the baby.'"

Now I wondered who Miss Leavtcher Seals was, and was she a doctor, but I knew mother was going to tell me if I just listened. It was so hard to hold back my questions and I really tried, but it just came out, and I said, "But Mother, what about a doctor? And who is Miss Leavtcher Seals? Was she the doctor?"

She looked at me and smiled again, touching me on my face and said, "Back then, colored people were not able to go to the hospital to have babies, and Miss Seals was a midwife."

Then I asked, "What's a midwife?"

Mother answered, "That's a person that delivered babies in your home like a doctor."

In my mind that meant we were too poor to pay for a doctor and a room in the hospital. I felt sad but happy, all at the same time. Sad, because colored people were deprived of many things that whites took for granted and happy because I was learning so much about our lives back in the day. This was very interesting to me, because it was history, and I was a part of that history.

≈

In my heart, I started to feel as though I was born in a special time, maybe even to a divine calling. It was like a cool breeze falling all over my body and I knew just at that moment in time that I was born to do something special. I wanted mother to tell me a lot more, and I asked her, "Why do white people hate colored people?"

Mother was surprised at my question, and put her arms around my petite body to calm the sadness that she saw in my eyes and heard in my voice, and said, "Just because we are different, that's all, baby."

My child's heart felt sadness to think that anyone would hate another because of outside looks. I found myself looking for peace inside of me to keep the spirit of love in my heart. So, I spoke a silent word to God, saying, *I can make a difference with your help.*

I knew that my parents were not educated, but they were very close to the spirit of God that guided them, and that is what helped them with raising all of us children. I hoped that same spirit would help me, as well.

We sat for hours it seemed, talking about my birth, and what I meant to my family. I found myself remembering that talk with my Big Daddy, but I kept silent and never said a word as mother continued with her story. She went on to say that after my father found the midwife, I was finally born on, November 25, 1947 at 4:30 p.m.

It was very exciting to see my birth record, showing all the vital information regarding the time and place of my birth. When I took a closer look at my birth records, it was interesting to find out that my father was listed as, "William McGhee a col. (meaning colored) man, twenty-two years old, born in Pike county, and worked at Red and White Store as a, 'Grocery Boy.'" That is the way it was spelled out on the official birth record. My mother was listed as, "Alberta Allen, a 'Housewife,' col., born in Pike county and twenty-two years of age." It listed me as their third child, and I found out that my mother was the sixth child born to Clarence Allen and Litta (Lydia) Neal, my grandparents. It was said back in the day that the storytellers were born in threes. I was the third child born to my parents. So, I started to believe that old saying, because I am a storyteller as well.

In my memory I can still see and feel my spirit in that small apartment in the Project of Burglund Town that all nine children and two parents occupied. We had three bedrooms, with what I remember as a large hallway, one bathroom, a storage room, a front living-room, and a kitchen with a big deep freezer in the corner.

I will never forget that deep freezer that always had lots of food inside. Many times we were all put in the car to go visit the people in the country, who were members of Daddy's church. They loved giving him food for all those babies, as Mother put it. Mother always said they never paid Daddy any salary, but they did give him a lot of food to keep him happy. We got so much food until sometimes I was

~

sad, because whenever Daddy came home with all that food—it seemed to be always in the summer time—we children couldn't play, because we all had to stay indoors to shell peas, shuck corn, or cut up okra for the deep freezer. I had lots of friends from school that lived in the Projects that wanted to play with me. They laughed at me at times because I had to stay indoors and work. I can remember times while cutting okra that I would daydream of that terrifying secret I held in my soul.

When I could go out to play, we had fun and played jump rope, hopscotch, and hide and seek, until Daddy would come home; then it was back to work.

My father was a Baptist preacher, and that was hard for a child to live with most of the time. We had church at home on Wednesday night, as well as every Sunday when he pastured. I never understood why my father pastured four churches. He took us to a different church every Sunday. I had fun going to church out in the country, and found many friends. The children would be so kind because we were the pastor's children. We also went sometimes to visit the members' homes, and they had lots of animals of all kinds. Some I liked, and others I was afraid to be near. I enjoyed the little chicks that we called, "Little Bitties."

I was sad when Daddy would ask my sister Lydia to sing, but wouldn't ever ask me. As much as I didn't want to admit it at the time, I just couldn't sing. Daddy tried us all out to be in his choir, but I sounded so bad, he would tell me to go stand by the door and pass out the church fans. My voice was so bad—and still is today—but I always wanted to sing so badly.

I had my very own girls' club, and it consisted of all the girls that lived in the Projects that I knew and played with me everyday when I could come outside. I was the president and would chair our Saturday meetings. We would talk about girl things like boys, dolls, and raising money for our club parties. We would plan parties with all the children on the block to play baseball, basketball, and hide and go seek. After we were done with our important business meeting, we played jump rope, hopscotch, and hide and go seek, until Daddy would come home. After our meetings, I would always have party food. I bought the food with my own money that I got for working at Mrs. Quinn's house, an elderly lady that took a liking to me, and asked me to come and help her clean her house on Saturdays. I loved Mrs. Quinn.

The town of McComb, Mississippi, was a big place to me as a child. As I remember, we lived right in the middle of the Projects, very near the school. The local store was also within walking distance from us. Down the back of our apartment ran what seemed at the time to be a long large road. Like so many other things in our childhood, that old road seemed so big to me, but today, it has gotten so very small.

My school, too, seemed so big to me as a child, and I loved going there. I don't understand why I liked school, because I didn't have very many friends since we were so poor.

≈

The children often made fun of me, and I just prayed a lot to become somebody great someday. I learned how to ignore them, to make sure they didn't make me mean and hard-hearted like they were inside.

My dad always told me, "Don't let them steal your joy."

As I grew, I found private time all alone to pray in my bedroom. I wanted to read, but I was having problems keeping up in class. The teacher gave us chapters to read in our reader every day, and we were told to be prepared to tell what the story was about the next day. It was hard to do the homework, because we didn't have anyone to help us. As much as I loved my Mom and Dad, I wish they had been better educated, so they could have helped us like the other children's parents did. So, I would go back to school the next day and ask my friends about the story in the chapter we had to read for homework.

There was one teacher—Mrs. Lula Kelly O'Neal— that I liked most of all, because she never hit me or called me stupid. I would love going into her class to learn things about life and taking care of your family, like cooking and making clothes. She said that I was smart, and that made me happy, because no one else treated me that way. I loved to stay in class during recess to comb her hair while she talked to me about life and made me feel good about myself. She knew I liked stories from back in the day, and she shared her own memories with me. In every way, I felt like she was my friend. She encouraged me to get involved in things that gave me a sense of self-worth. I took her advice, and joined many school organizations like the 4H, drama, debating club, and the band.

I even became a radio host for my dad's radio talk show that aired on Sunday mornings for the folks who were too sick to go to church. I became so happy doing this, because it gave me more friends, and made me feel proud—a feeling I rarely had outside of my mother's embrace. People in the community started calling me a star, and I smiled a lot more than before. It was taking my mind off the fear I carried inside.

Yes, this time in my life was interesting, all right, what with me starting to grow up and think about my life as an adult. The storytelling was always a pleasure, and still is. To this day, I love to sit down with my mother, who is still beautiful and striking. Time and again, I will ask her, "Mother, will you please tell me about the day I was born?"

And she'll always smile and reply, "Well, On November 24, 1947, a little before midnight, you wanted to be born. It was a cold windy night and I went into labor with you inside of me kicking and raising habit wanting to be born..."

This story is an inspired fiction...a fictional account of a young woman whose life was influenced by stories she had been told as a young girl growing up in Mississippi. Those stories have taken on a new life in the mind of the author, and watch the characters come alive in your mind as well. This work is also influenced by actual research into family genealogy discovered as she tried to understand feelings she had felt all of her life. The story is uniquely told in the form of flashbacks and memories that came to her as she began to put the story on paper.

PROLOGUE

In California, there lived a family labeled "Mulatto." Jack and Tyara Nordstrom, and their six children— Little T, Jack Jr., Ronald, Ennis, Sylvia, and Emily— lived in a beautiful home overlooking a golf course.

Mr. Nordstrom was a professional golfer, and his wife an author. She believed in the African Oral History Tradition of Story Telling. She became a story-teller herself. She had a secret hidden in her spirit, which she planned to tell her children someday.

Bedtime was a special time for the couple. Tyara loved lying in bed and talking to her husband about her past. One warm, clear night in early November, she decided to tell her husband about her dreams. She still carried fear from her childhood, fear from the secrets of her family she had learned through storytelling.

"When I was a child I loved going to visit my Big Daddy at least once a month with my parents and brother," she said.

"On Sundays after church, my father always took us to visit our grandparents. Big Daddy would be sitting on the porch with his legs stretched out across the banister, smoking his pipe as always. I sat down

under his legs many times to hear his story telling."
Then she asked, "You know what?"

"What?" her husband answered.

"My family didn't have a lot of money back in
those days, but mother always told us that we were
rich in love," she replied.

"I'm glad you felt that your family was loved during that horrible time in our history," he said.

"My Big Daddy said many of our relatives passed
for white to get equal rights," she sighed as the
memories played through in her mind. Her husband just held her in his arms and listened as she
went on and on about her family secrets.

"Rich in love, that's a great thought," he finally said,
as they both drifted off to sleep. She began to dream
with flashbacks into her past. Her dream flashed.

> "Sir, stop! You may damage the merchandise," a
> man said firmly as he reached down and picked up
> the beautiful, thin, half-white, half-colored slave
> girl from the floor. Tyara thrashed in her sleep.
> "Look daughter, you can't tell anyone that he is
> passing for white. If you do, the whole family could
> be killed as they sleep," a man's voice threatened.

Tyara moaned as the dreams plagued her.

"Look they are coming! The house is on fire!" she
screamed, coming out of her dream.

"No, no! Help, help!"

She was having that same nightmare that frightened her so much. She jumped into the arms of her husband, crying.

"Honey, please help me! It's happening all over again! That dream seems to be so real," she said.

He held her in his arms and said the sweetest words to comfort her as always. "I'm here my love. It was just a dream, so go back to sleep."

She looked into his eyes and said, "I must find a way to clear my mind of this fear inside of me. I will start by writing it, putting it all down on paper to free my soul."

"That's my girl, you know the best way to clear yourself from all fear is to face it head on. You write your best stories from your inner soul. Sharing that pain will free you and help others," he said as he smiled.

She felt stronger after they talked and decided to face her fears. Jack encouraged her to write the story in a book and she agreed as she drifted back to sleep.

The next day she remembered what her husband had said about facing her past head on, and she found the courage to start her task by writing it all down on paper. She wrote about stories her Big Daddy had told her about her ancestors when she was a child. While writing, she started to daydream about her childhood. Those stories were fixed in her soul. Her oral history came to life in her mind as she wrote her story, her mind drifting back in time...

CHAPTER I

I felt strange, and a voice spoke to me. "Close your mind to the world and relax," it said to me. An uplifting feeling came over me. Something very strange was happening. At first, I thought I was getting sleepy or maybe even sick. I could not stop thoughts from coming into my head. Then I realized that I wasn't afraid—I was going to the plantation to find out the truth about my past. The next thing I knew, I drifted away. I heard a voice, it grew faint as it called to me, "Harry...H...a...r...r...y."

Right away, I heard someone calling out to some one, and I thought they were calling me, but it was the wrong name. Finally I understood the name: Harry!

Who's Harry? I wondered.

A force was pulling on my body and I felt myself flying through thin air. When it stopped, I was wearing clothes that reminded me of things people wore back in the day. It was made out of a potato sack material, which scratched my skin when I walked, but I had to get use to it, because I had nothing else. Walking through a beautiful but undeveloped town, I found myself in a large crowd of screaming people.

It was so strange to me to see people all in the

streets like a celebration, they had the old wooden boxes set up like tables to look like a counter, and big pieces of wooden board nailed up on the side of the building as a roster for everybody to sign in their slaves that was for sell.

I noticed the date: the 27th day of November, 1809. That's when I knew that I was back in time. I thought to myself, *What is all the screaming about?*

I looked up to see a large sign that read: "Slave Auction: Slaves for Sale."

I noticed something that looked like a stage. As I moved closer to see what it really was, I walked through the crowd but touched no one. Finding that strange, I reached out to touch the man next to me.

"Excuse me, sir, can you please tell me where I am?" I asked, but I noticed he couldn't hear me, see me, or even feel my touch. He just kept on talking to his two friends. I then got an idea.

I will stay next to them and learn more information about their lives. I will name them based on the color of the shirts they are wearing, "Black, White, and Gray."

They were doing a lot of talking about the slaves that came on the block to be brought, and I was getting a lot of history about the people that lived in this town, so I stayed and listened. I looked around and realized that no one in the crowd was able to see me. No other women were there except for slave women, and they were standing in line near the stage to be sold.

I realized that I was there to watch. Everyone was

looking at the white men with black whips in their hands. They stood on a platform, built to raise the slave people high enough so that the crowd could see everyone on display for sale. Then I noticed the Podium, it looked hand made by the way it was built for the speakers selling slaves.

The auction opened, and the first slave to be sold was pushed onto the platform by one of the big men holding a black whip. She was pushed so hard that she fell down. Seeing her fall, the white man started to hit her with the whip. I wanted to stop him, so I ran up on the platform. But I could do nothing.

When I looked up, a handsome white man had jumped onto the stage. He grabbed the big man, holding him by the arm with a strong grip.

"Sir, stop! You may damage the merchandise," he said firmly.

He reached down and picked up a beautiful, thin, half-white, half-colored slave girl from the floor. She appeared more white-skinned than black. I knew without a doubt that she was connected to me; she looked so much like family. A wonderful feeling came over me. Standing close, I looked into her eyes. She was beautiful; her eyes were green and she had long black hair. She was so pretty that I couldn't keep my eyes off of her, nor could I understand this business of selling people, and it made me so sad.

I could tell that she was my relative all right. She had wide-set eyes and high, rounded cheekbones. Her skin looked as white as any white person there, but she was being sold as a slave. The only thing that identified her as a colored girl was her hair, which was black and curly. I noticed that all the slaves' skin colors differed. Some were dark and some were light. Some even looked white.

The auction began. It was very loud and it seemed unorganized to me, although the white men seemed to know exactly what they were doing. All the men in charge carried long black whips. They hit the colored people on their backs to get them in some kind of order for display.

Then one of the men near me started talking, "I noticed there are plantation owners from all across the southern states here to buy them a slave," said the man in the black shirt, whom I gave the name Black.

Slave-buying auctions were big business in the South. Slave owners were bidding for slaves as if buying furniture for their homes. It sounded like a sports competition with all of the white men pushing and yelling at slaves. They were there to make purchases.

When they got things in order, they pushed the beautiful mulatto girl onto the display area. It was staged almost like a fashion show. She wore a soft white dress, through which men could see the shadow of her body. On her feet, she wore what looked like white ballet slippers. Her breasts were the size of a mature woman, even though her face showed she could not have been more than twelve years old. When she stood up on the stage, everyone stopped talking to gaze at her.

≈

Her beauty was absolutely electrifying. She was the most beautiful girl that I had seen in a long time. She appeared to be quite shy and frightened. I wanted to run up on stage to take her home and protect her, but it was impossible. I was only there to watch.

"Emily Allen! Date of Birth, November 27, 1793!" one of the men yelled.

I thought, as they called out her specifications, *Oh my goodness, she is being sold on her birthday,*

It was strange; looking at Emily, a girl I knew must be my great-great-grandmother, who looked so young, innocent, and alive. I couldn't believe it. I was standing in front of her when she was just a girl. I thought, *What an exciting feeling this is.*

I found myself trying to take Emily in my arms to protect her, but then again nothing happened. I kept forgetting I was only there to watch. Then the auction started.

"We'll start the bidding for this fine, young colored woman at $100!" The auctioneer shouted. I was surprised. I knew that $100 was rather expensive for a slave.

These white men were taken by Emily's beauty and they all wanted her. They kept bidding and bidding until the price was sky-high. The bids began to sound like a countdown; each time it went up, one plantation owner dropped out. Soon only three men were left in the contest for Emily.

"Three-fifty!" shouted Master William Clifton Carson.

≈

Then the man I called Gray said, "Old Carson raises sheep on his plantation. He need strong slaves, what you think he wants with the little thing?" And he laughed.

They all thought that was so funny, I just watched them picking fun at everyone and was as quiet as a mouse. It was good for me to learn as much at I could while I was standing near them. They couldn't see me any way.

"Four hundred!" countered Frederick Alexander Montgomery, Jr.

"Look at Montgomery, a cattle rancher. Did you all know that he is married to William Carson's sister?" said the man I called White.

"Yah, that old hound, rumors has it that the Carson and Montgomery families had a falling out after Frederick and Helen got married, and you see the feud didn't help the bidding," said the man I called Black.

"Four-fifty," yelled Mr. Carson.

"He knows he can't afford to bid any higher, but he hate to let Montgomery win her because of their fight years ago," said White.

"Four-Seventy-Five!"

The latest bid from Montgomery forced Carson out of the race.

"Five hundred!"

The newest bid came from the only bidder left besides Carson and Montgomery.

"Oh look, my friends. Edward Dennis Hoover Jr., his old man died and gave him the plantation. They raise horses. He married Montgomery's sister Charlotte," said Gray.

Oh, now I understand...since Mr. Montgomery saw that his brother-in-law wanted this slave badly, he yielded his bid to him for a future favor that he knew would come in handy one day.

"Man look the bidding stopped at $500. That pretty little thing sold for the highest price ever," said White.

When he said that, my memory started to come pouring into my head, and all of a sudden I felt as though I had been born there. I became a part of this time period in that very moment with knowledge that I realized came into me from a very strong power. I didn't feel lost or strange any more. I found myself knowing everyone's name, but they still couldn't hear me or feel my touch.

Master Edward D. Hoover was the man who had saved Emily from the whip. I watched Mr. Hoover's face carefully. I could tell by remembering my oral stories that winning the bid pleased him. He wanted to raise Emily as a white girl, because he knew his wife had an illness that could stop her from having children.

He looked very pleased about winning the bid for Emily.

The oral stories stated Mr. Hoover wasn't in love with his wife. But they were good friends, and as they grew up they became best friends. Their fathers put them together to keep their families strong. I could read his face when he was looking at Emily;

$\sim$

he was wondering how he was going to keep anyone from knowing that she was colored, because
she could pass for white—through deceit as the oral
stories stated that he thought, *I'll cross that bridge
when I get to it.*

I decided that I would be part of the Hoover family while I was there, so I followed them from the
auction to the plantation. Just as we were leaving, I
heard Master Montgomery's voice.

"You owe me a favor, you know. I gave you that
bid."

Master Hoover just nodded his head as he walked
out to get into his carriage. I walked with them to
his fine horse carriage. He was especially kind to his
new slave. We all got in the horse carriage, and I
watched Master Hoover put his arms around Emily
as if she was his daughter. He had a blanket in the
carriage, which he wrapped around her shoulders
because she was shivering in her thin dress.

Soon I noticed a light-complexioned man. He
looked like the brother of one of the plantation owners, but he drove the horses. I heard Master Hoover
call him Harry. I found myself moving to the front
of the carriage with him, remembering the name I'd
heard calling me into the past. I knew that I wanted
to know more about this man. I stared into his face as
Master Hoover told Harry to drive us to the ranch.

Our family history states that when Master
Hoover's father died at the age of seventy-two, Master Hoover became the youngest slave owner in that

part of the South. Also Harry was half-white, the son of William Carson, Sr., and a slave named Sara. After Mr. Carson died, his wife, who'd found out about his indiscretions and didn't approve, sold Sara to Master Hoover's father. Sara was pregnant with Harry at the time, so he was born on the Hoover ranch and had lived there for forty years. I noticed that Harry was looking at Emily with a very interesting desire to get to know her better, and Master Hoover noticed it too.

When we got to the ranch, Emily looked more relaxed and seemed to be less afraid of Master Hoover. He had held her in his arms all the way to the ranch, and he was talking to her about the way things operated on the Hoover Ranch Plantation.

"We're home now, Emily," said Master Hoover and gently said,

"I want you to think of this ranch as your home, now and forever." I moved back next to Emily in the carriage.

"You are only allowed to work inside the big house and not around the field slaves," he said and continued. "You'll be the nanny to my children. You'll live in the nanny's quarters, which are part of the big house."

Actually, as I looked the house was set up with two nanny's quarters: one inside the house, used while the nanny was breast-feeding, and the other outside, next to the house and connected to the porch so that the nanny would have easy access to

∾

the children. I think this was done to keep her from actually living in the main part of the big house when the children were over two years old. I notice he was going on and on,

"Your job will be to look after the children's needs at all times," he explained. "They'll call you 'Mama.' We raise horses here at the ranch. We sell them on the market. We've got fifty slaves living here and they take care of the horses and the rest of the plantation. You see the quarters over near the barn? That's where Willie stays. He's in charge of the health of the horses."

"Willie and Harry have been on this ranch for decades. They are in charge of the slaves who took care of exercising the horses, and the slaves who fed and cleaned the horses. We've got ten other slaves to take care of the grounds and plant food in the garden," continued Master Hoover.

I found myself getting tired of his story telling to Emily, but she seem very alert in knowing everything, and he went on.

"We raise our own food. You'll like it here. We've got greens, tomatoes, okra, potatoes, beans, corn, peas, watermelon, and fruit trees."

He told her that the slaves did all the planting and picking of food from the garden. Harry was in charge of the other slaves and the horse carriage, and he was the family's driver. Known to the community as Harry Carson, most of the white community thought he was the paid overseer of the Hoover

~

plantation. This made me very sad for the slave people. He kept on informing her.

"We raise our own chickens, ducks, pigs, and cows. We even have a fishpond to catch fresh fish for dinner. Besides the livestock, we've got pets: dogs, birds, and cats."

Then I heard him say, "Twenty of the slaves are women; ten keep the quarters clean, take care of their children, and help prepare the food from the garden for the winter. They work every day except Sunday. See now, over there's the church. All day Sunday, the slaves have church and celebrations. I supervised Harry and Willie along with other field slaves to build the church on the plantation," Feeling proud of himself.

It was nice, and it looked like it could seat over 100 people.

I thought to myself, *Emily should be tired of the lesson, but she isn't.* He went on and on.

"Master Montgomery and Master Carson bring their families and slaves every Sunday to visit Hoover Ranch. The slave women and the children ride in big horse buggies, and the men walk, or hang onto the sides of the buggies. The guards ride horses next to the slave buggies to make sure no one tries to run away."

He stopped, smiled, and looked into her eyes. Emily smiled back at him and he continued.

"They spend the whole day every Sunday celebrating a week's work done. The slaves believe that God is the reason for their good health. He enriches their work and they praise Him every week for it. Dressed in their Sunday best, they all praise God, sing, and dance the whole day. We have our own celebration in the big house as we watch them and listen to the good singing by Sister Harriet. She is a great singer. You know, our ranch is known for having happy niggers. The guards are here mainly to keep out strangers who might be snooping around for information about our private lives. Our family is very cautious about what goes on here. Nobody's allowed to leave this place unless I say so," said Master Hoover.

I sat there listening to this man with all that power to run people's lives, and it made me love and appreciate my ancestors even more for the things they went through to pave the way for us, as he went on with his lesson to Emily.

"I'm protecting you. You know that! I've got to guard my private life and my slaves," he said and continued pouring out his soul to Emily.

"I gave them orders they should shoot to kill anyone they find trespassing on my property. If anyone comes through that gate without permission, I told 'em to shoot first and ask questions later. But they aren't here on account of the slaves, because I got good niggers."

I saw guards with guns surrounded the plantation gates.

Master Hoover wasn't telling Emily everything. I started remembering the storytelling my grandfather told me about them while he was going on and on about Emily's duties. One thing he never mentioned to her was the HMC Club. The club, which was named HMC for Hoover, Montgomery, and Carson, was started by the slave owners. If a member of the three families wanted a person elimi-nated, a meeting of the HMC was called and they helped each other do the job. They had control of the community because they were owners of almost everything in town. They influenced the sheriff and the business owners, who paid the HMC Club to let them stay in business. Anyone that got in their way was removed and never seen or found again.

On Sundays, the HMC Club would spend the day together in the big house. They had their own church service and dressed in their best attire. The club members and their families sat on the porch while Sister Harriet, a slave woman, would sing those good old gospel hymns. Sister Harriet was very spiri-tual and none of the masters had any sexual deal-ings with her because they feared her praying a bad spell on them and their families.

There was something unholy about the HMC Club. Master William Carson, Sr., had started gam-bling games, betting his slaves. These games were played with slave people as if they were animals, and the HMC Club had them about twice a month. They called it "The Climaxing First Game." A slave master picked two strong male field slaves and two female field slaves, then used them in a sex game, taking bets and bringing in big money. The slaves were forced to have sex in front of a group of white men that paid money to see this show. It lasted all day and sometimes all night by candlelight.

The couples started out fully dressed in the center of the barn.

"Let's go, get ready, and let the games begin!" Master Carson always started his game the same way I was told. At the signal, the slaves were to start kissing and touching each other. They'd take off one piece of clothing after the next until they were completely undressed. The crowd cheered them on. It was all part of the show. Once the white men made their choice and set their bids, it was recorded in writing and couldn't be changed. To win, the white men had to predict which couple finished first.

If the slaves didn't perform, they could be killed, and they knew it; they'd heard that Master William Carson, Sr., had a couple killed once. When they didn't obey the rules, he up and killed them right in front of everyone. Master's orders.

Harry was part of the family from birth, and up until this time was treated like a white man. Emily and Master Hoover still sat in the carriage with Harry not saying a word until now.

"Isn't she a might young to be a nanny?" asked Harry gently.

This was the moment the friendship between these two men changed. Master Hoover noticed that Harry was showing an interest in Emily.

"Mind your own business," he snapped. Master

Hoover looked Harry in the eye. "Don't you go near Emily unless I tell you to," he muttered.

Emily heard them arguing about her and began to feel upset. I could see her fear coming back. Master Hoover slipped his arm around her.

"You stay clear of Harry. For that matter, don't you go near the field slaves, none of them." He went on a bit to make his point.

After he finished talking to her, he got out of the carriage and helped her down. Harry's feelings were hurt and he did not talk anymore after that, he just turned and went to work. He cleaned the horses up and took them to eat. I got very tired and restless, so I decided to take a look around the grounds, which were so pretty. The trees and grass were as green as emeralds.

Soon I found myself running through the fields like a child, heading toward the horse stables. I had wanted a horse ever since I was very young and the Hoover horses were the best-looking horses I'd ever seen. It was like looking into a picture book of beautiful horses. They had rippling muscles in their chests, proud flaring nostrils, with a soft bright coat of hair, and long silky tails.

I guess that is why the Hoover Ranch Plantation's reputation was so good. The slave children fed the horses and adults groomed them. Hoover Ranch was known as the best horse ranch in that part of the South.

The big house was beautiful too. It was white, trimmed in gray with a very pretty porch wrapped around it painted in white. The Master could stand there to oversee the slaves, and the house sat on a hill covered with pretty green grass surrounded by flowers of many colors over looking the valley. There were some little houses built out back of the big house that looked like small dollhouses. The little houses were built for the slaves' quarters. They were all painted white and looked very neat, miniatures of the big house.

I was so wrapped up it the beauty of it all and didn't notice them after they got out of the carriage and walked to the door of the big house. So, I ran to catch up to them.

Master Hoover stood talking to Madam Charlotte at the front door of the mansion. She opened the door for Emily.

I noticed Emily and Madam Charlotte look deep into each other's eyes, as though they wanted to be a part of each other's lives. I still didn't fully understand what was going on with these two women. While we were standing at the door, I looked at Madam Charlotte Hoover and thought, *What a stunningly beautiful woman she is, she seems sweet and gentle, too*...which I soon found out she was unless she couldn't get her way. Then she was a force of power around the ranch.

Master Hoover seemed surprised at the way Charlotte took to Emily—almost as though she wanted her for a daughter. It was true that Emily could pass for white, which is what he really wanted. Master Hoover knew his wife might never have a child of her own because she had an illness that made child-birth dangerous for her.

When I looked inside the big house I noticed it was exquisite. The furniture looked antique as if it came from a long time ago. They had no toilet; instead there was an outhouse behind the house. Old kerosene lamps, made out of brass and glass, shone bright light into the room.

Madam Charlotte and Master Hoover whispered to each other.

"A nanny? She can't nurse our babies until she has a baby herself," Madam Charlotte said.

"She'll have a baby with one of the slaves, maybe Harry," Master Hoover said trying to fool her, thinking he'd impregnate her himself.

"She looks like a baby herself! She's too young to bear children. I won't let any man touch her at all until she's older." Madam Charlotte saw that her husband was about to object so she put her foot down.

"If we're going to keep her here at Hoover Ranch, that's how it's going to be. This girl is too young to be a nanny and if you don't like it you can take her back to the auction right now and sell her for an older woman."

She saw tears running down Emily's face.

Then she thought of a reason to put off getting pregnant herself; she wanted to raise Emily before thinking of having her own child. She said,

∽

"Furthermore, I don't think we should start our family just yet, because we still need to wait until Dr. Pitts give us that new medication for me to start, which would be about the time she would be ready to have children."

Madam Charlotte knew her talk about sending Emily back to the auction had upset her. She felt bad about hurting Emily's feelings, but it had to be done in order to get Master Hoover to see things her way. Then she put her arms around Emily's little body to comfort her. Emily seemed to like Madam Charlotte from the start, and she wanted desperately to stay on the ranch. When she noticed she had won the fight, she continued. "I'll take her in," said Madam Charlotte, "but only as my own child for now, as if I gave birth to her. You work out the details."

Just at that moment she remembered his story about the girl he met in boarding school in Chicago. Seeing the look on Master Hoover's face, she thought he hoped for something else with Emily, and what that was she wasn't sure.

"I will take care of her for four years, until she is old enough to become a nanny," said Madam Charlotte firmly.

She was thinking that by then Emily would be ready to marry and have her own children. Master Hoover seemed confused and a bit unhappy, but he knew he really didn't have a choice if he wanted to have Emily some day for himself—he had to go with her plans. His wife laid down the law about the care of Emily and what was going to take place.

Madam Charlotte wanted to take care of Emily and she turned to Miss Lilly, her housemaid, who was taking Emily to her room for a bath and said,

"I will raise this child as if she were my own daughter. I don't want her to end up like Sweet Anna."

"I understand, Madam. Sweet Anna lived on the Montgomery Plantation, and she is used for sex by all of the masters in the club any time they want it. That's how she got her name, Sweet Anna. She is known as every man's bed warmer," replied Miss Lilly.

"You are right, and I think it would be wrong to put Emily out with the field slaves for the taking," she said to Miss Lilly and in a very low voice.

"And maybe Master Hoover's use as well."

Miss Lilly didn't dare comment, she just nodded and kept on with her work, and Madam Charlotte just kept on talking to her.

"I've picked Harry to father Emily's children when she is ready. Harry is a mulatto slave, treated like a white man here on Hoover's ranch, even perceived as a white, free man—the foreman—by the majority of the community. He doesn't work like the field slaves—he is their boss. Master Hoover leaves him in charge because he trusts him. He would make a fine husband too," she concluded.

What Madam Charlotte didn't know, although she thought it, was that her husband bought Emily for one reason: to become a bed warmer for himself.

~

She didn't know that Emily's beauty fascinated him to that extent.

"According to her papers, she's sixteen years old," said his wife.

Master Hoover—oblivious to his wife's conversation with her housemaid—hopefully interrupted. "Sixteen-year-old slave girls are having babies and marrying, if they are healthy. She looks plenty healthy and old enough to take on her duties."

"Stop right there Edward," Madam Charlotte wouldn't have any more of this talk,

"Emily is no more than twelve years old, by looking at her small little body. And even if she were sixteen, she isn't big enough to have any children, or get married. If you keep this up you can take her back to the auction and swap her for someone older. Or go by the new rules—let's raise her like a white child and she can marry Harry when she is older. I'm not letting any man take advantage of a child."

That was right up his ally, so she thought she'd won the argument. Master Hoover let Madam Charlotte do whatever she wanted for now. He had his master plan in place for Emily from the start and he wanted her badly. He'd wait if he had to, but he was determined to have her. Emily was a pretty girl. He knew that in a few years she would be a magnificent woman and beautiful.

Madam Charlotte liked the fact that Emily could pass for white because she had wanted a daughter for so many years and now she felt she had one.

~

During the next four years, Madam Charlotte teamed up with Miss Lilly, her housemaid and cook, to teach Emily about the things she need to know to pass for white and become their daughter. They taught her well. They taught her everything that she needed to know, or everything a young girl should know before getting married. It was fun watching them change this young girl into a well-mannered woman. They taught her how to cook, clean, speak properly, read, and how to be a proper wife. Emily became an accomplished young lady.

Madam Charlotte had the nanny's quarters inside the house turned into what looked like a classroom. This was where Emily learned to read, and it was also where she slept.

A secret book was passed among the relatives in Madam Charlotte's family, called *Sex Can Be Exciting and Good in Marriage*. Madam Charlotte had gotten it from her sister-in-law, Helen, who received the book from a relative who lived in England. Madam Charlotte and Emily read the book together.

Miss Lilly told sister Harriet about the soon to be marriage between Emily the new girl and Harry on the place, and in no time all the slaves on the plantation and their friends were talking about the big wedding that would take place when Emily turned twenty.

"Miss Lilly," called Madam Charlotte.

"Yes, Madam?" she hurried into the room.

"How did the slave learn about Emily's wedding to Harry?"

"Oh, I am sorry, Madam, I didn't know it was a secret."

"Well, in the future, keep what goes on in this house in this house. Now go back to work," she said in anger.

"Yes, Madam." Miss Lilly left the room.

Madam Charlotte made a rule that Emily was not allowed anywhere near Harry until her debut, which was just fine with Master Hoover. He had what he told himself was a "master plan." For four years, the only times Emily saw Harry were through the window as he came and went with Master Hoover.

Master Hoover tried to go into Emily's room many times late at night, but Madam Charlotte always caught him.

"I heard a noise, or "I just wanted to say goodnight." he'd say.

"Hmmm. Well, Emily can't be disturbed because she has an early morning class tomorrow," Madam Charlotte would reply.

His wife always seemed to be watching him and it made him angry, but Master Hoover would just go back to his library and read.

~

CHAPTER 2

November 26, 1813, was the day Master Hoover had anxiously awaited for four long years. Emily was coming out from the protection of her adopted mother, and he was ready. Her coming-out party was on her birthday, the anniversary of the day Emily was put up for sale.

Madam Charlotte thought that Emily's coming-out party was to be the day before her wedding, which she had already arranged. Emily's debut would be a noisy celebration with music, dancing, and lots of food, held in the big house. She invited Harry, the only slave allowed, who was passing for white.

Master Hoover was not happy about Harry, but he was happy about the four years being over. He ached to touch Emily. What he didn't know was that Madam Charlotte had a master plan of her own.

Years earlier, after Frederick Montgomery married Helen Carson, the Montgomery and Carson families had a falling out; the young owners managed to learn how to work together in business. Everyone talked about how old Master Carson had cheated Master Montgomery, Sr., out of a bid at the auction once, and Master Montgomery never forgave him.

Their friendship had ended right then and there, but the future generations decided it was foolish to keep it up, and started doing business together again. But the resulting feud interfered with a romance between Helen Carson's brother Percy and Frederick Montgomery's sister Charlotte. She was in love with Percy at that time, but their parents stopped them from getting married. Percy was in love with Charlotte when they were teenagers and had asked her to marry him when they were older, but her father wouldn't hear of his daughter marrying a Carson, not after the feud started. He put a stop to it right away by arranging a marriage with Master Hoover. This deeply upset Percy, so he left Mississippi and hadn't come back since.

Master Hoover had been waiting four years for this night; however, Madam Charlotte had been waiting ever since she was a teenager to be with the love of her life.

A few days before Emily's coming out party, Helen dropped by the house to see Charlotte.

"Percy will be in town," confided her sister-in-law, Helen. "I have a secret for you! He is planning to see you at Emily's coming-out party, if you'll just send him an invitation. You know he is still in love with you Charlotte."

"Oh my, Helen, don't say that! But please keep it between us, because I am also still in love with him. Edward and I are more like friends...he is still

in love with the girl he met at boarding school."
Charlotte replied.

"Oh, Charlotte, I am sorry. But now that Percy
is back and this can be our secret, okay?" Helen
replied.

"Okay," answered Madam Charlotte, intending
to put her master plan in motion that night.

It was almost time for the party and everyone
was busy. The Hoovers invited all of their friends to
attend this monumental event. On the invitations
that were sent out was Master Hoover's master plan,
full of lies.

"My sister from Virginia will be here and we're
throwing a party for her," Master Hoover told people. Of course, in his plan, Emily was his "sister."

"Why are you telling everyone that?" Madam
Charlotte had asked Master Hoover.

"This is the news for the community," he'd said.
"It's my way of protecting Emily's future. She'll pass
for white if she needs to."

Most of their friends knew the truth and would
never tell anyone anything different, but they wanted
to put this story out into the community so they
could pass Emily as white. Outside of the Hoover
Plantation, Emily's ethnicity was kept a secret, except
for close friends. Keeping secrets for each other was
part of their vows in the HMC Club.

Madam Charlotte bought a stunning green dress
for Emily to wear. It fit her waistline and draped
down to the floor, showing off her body's shape.

Outside, in the ballroom, Harry was looking handsome as he waited and wondered how his lovely bride was going to look, even though he knew that this was part of Master Hoover's master plan for Emily. "You'll never get close to her," Master Hoover had informed him.

But Harry would have to wait just a bit longer before he could look at Emily, because she wanted one last talk with Madam Charlotte. It was important to her to have this talk before her party.

Madam Charlotte went into Emily's room for their last talk. Emily stood in the doorway, electrifying in that floor length, emerald dress. Madam Charlotte sat down to talk. Emily had grown into a lovely young woman and she was ready to start her job as nanny. As she looked at her, Madam Charlotte felt so proud—just like a mother would look at her daughter.

"You look beautiful, dear," she said as Emily smoothed her skirts. She sat next to Madam Charlotte and when she began to talk, Emily spoke from her heart.

"I want to thank you for being like a mother to me," she said softly. "That was a lucky day for me, a little slave girl, when Master Hoover bought me from that auction and you decided to raise me as your daughter. When he brought me to this ranch, and to a new mother, my life became worth living."

Madam Charlotte was happy to hear Emily say those nice things to her. But Emily wasn't done yet.

~

"It's time for me to take care of the beautiful Hoover children that you're going to have," said Emily, smiling gently.

As Emily spoke, Madam Charlotte began to cry softly with tears running down her face she reached out for Emily's hand, and said,

"Emily, you are the daughter that I wanted many years ago, and thought I couldn't have."

Emily smiled, happy that they felt such affection for each other, and then they hugged. At last, they were ready to go into the party room to meet all of the Hoover's friends who were waiting to meet his "sister" Emily.

Harry, Master Hoover, and all their friends waited expectantly in the banquet hall. The door opened at the top of the stairs and Madam Charlotte came down. Everyone stopped and looked at her. She was exquisite. Suddenly, she stopped at the bottom of the stairs, surprised by the sight of her childhood sweetheart, Percy Carson, who was standing in attendance as if he was there to pick her up for a date. Even though she had invited him, she didn't think he would really come.

When Madam Charlotte pulled herself together, she looked into her friends' faces, and said, "Ladies and gentlemen, please look this way." She paused dramatically. "I am honored to present and introduce you to Emily Allen, my sister-in-law from Virginia!"

Like a vision, Emily appeared at the top of the stairs. The room immediately silenced and the guests gazed at her beauty. She walked down the stairs elegantly, like a queen. Master Hoover was stunned speechless; he could not keep his eyes off of Emily. He stared at her all night, even while he was dancing in the arms of his own wife.

As they danced closely, an odd look was on Madam Charlotte's face. I could see she was feeling the Master's body heat next to her. He was aroused, but what she didn't know was he was watching Emily behind her back. Madam Charlotte started to become aroused herself from the feeling of his body touching hers. She wanted to leave the party for a few minutes to make love with him, just to hide the fact that she still loved Percy. She thought he saw her looking at Percy with love in her eyes.

"We have all night to be together," he whispered. "If we leave the room it might upset Emily. After all, this is her first party. She needs our support, don't you think?" he asked.

"Yes, you're right my dear," she said, thinking it was good that he was pleased and cooperating with her plans. Still dancing, Madam Charlotte took the opportunity to talk to Master Hoover about Emily and Harry's future.

"I want to thank you for your approval of Harry's marriage to Emily," she began. "Emily will make him a good wife."

When she said that, I could tell that she was

going on too much about Harry and Emily. Master Hoover was starting to get jealous, and pretty soon I was afraid he'd be boiling with anger. Madam Charlotte seemed to notice, and wanted to test him.

"Edward, isn't this wonderful?

"What?" he asked.

"When Emily and Harry are married tomorrow, they'll be part of our family!" She replied. Her words about Harry being part of the family made him angry and he stopped dancing.

"It's *not* wonderful. Harry will never be a part of us," he snorted and said.

"Harry is a slave on the ranch, he works here, and that's all."

"Sshhh! You're making a scene in front of everyone," said Madam Charlotte.

"And furthermore—"

"Could you join me in the library?" she interrupted him because she didn't want anyone to hear, but I followed. When they reached the library, he exploded.

"No more! Scene or no scene, I've gone along with you too long!" He was beginning to raise his voice. She was trying to get him to lower his voice, and he did, but he was furious. "Four years I've put up with your ideas, just because I paid a lot of money for that slave," he hissed.

I was just as shocked as Madam Charlotte. I think he was jealous of Harry being able to put his hands on Emily while they were dancing.

∼

"Edward, Emily's wedding is tomorrow, and you are going to spoil it for her if you keep on acting this way in front of our friends," said Madam Charlotte.

"I don't give a flying you know what about friends. This has got to stop! It's gone on long enough." Master Hoover's voice carried right through the library door.

Everyone at the party stopped dancing. They were surprised at what was going on. None of it made any sense to anyone. Madam Charlotte was speechless, stunned into a state of shock. He was just going on and on.

"If my father knew about this, I know he would be turning over in his grave!" Master Hoover started to the door. "This stops now! I want Emily out of this house tonight and put in the nanny's quarters out back, where she belongs." He started to walk off, but changed his mind. "I want her moved before I get back home tonight. She'll stay there until she is needed in the nanny's quarters in the main house." He paused as he approached the door. "You know, I feel the presence of my father's spirit in this room and he is not pleased with me at all."

Everyone, including Emily and Harry, heard him arguing with Madam Charlotte. No one knew what they were arguing about, but they really wanted to know. They couldn't hear the exact words because Madam Charlotte had closed the door to protect their privacy. The party stopped and everyone stood around with surprised looks on their faces.

∼

"Get the horse and carriage. I'm going into town," said Master Hoover abruptly. He was talking to Harry. There was silence for a moment.

Madam Charlotte was in the library crying. Emily heard her and went in to see about her, and when she passed by Master Hoover standing in the foyer waiting for the carriage to come around, Emily's eyes showed fear. Master Hoover looked angry. He couldn't look at Emily. He knew that he had strong feelings for her; he feared that his deep sexual feelings might be aroused. As she passed by him, he smelled the scent of her body, and it was very sensuous to him. Her tempting aroma caused him to get aroused all over again and he quickly moved into another room to get his mind on something else.

Master Hoover was highly susceptible and influenced by Emily's beauty. The smell of her body turned on the indulgence of his appetite, and he wanted her badly.

Everyone seemed to think that the argument was about Madam Charlotte's old boyfriend because of the affectionate look she'd given him when she first saw him. Master Hoover hadn't even seen Madam Charlotte look at Percy Carson because he was too busy thinking about Emily and watching for her to appear.

I think Madam Charlotte may have worried that he'd seen her and she thought maybe that upset him. After all, a good-looking man like Percy Carson would make any man jealous. He was tall, had dark brown hair and gray eyes, and was dressed to impress.

∼

All the food was still in the kitchen. Miss Lilly was waiting in the kitchen to serve the food, but no one got a chance to eat. I watched Master Hoover when he went into the kitchen to talk to Miss Lilly.

"Put the food away," he told her.

When she looked surprised, he grew impatient.

"I said, put it away. Use it for the big celebration in the slave quarters tomorrow," he replied.

She noticed he didn't say wedding, he said celebration. He knew something was going to happen to interfere with the wedding between Harry and Emily, but he wasn't telling anyone.

"Help get Emily moved to the outside nanny's quarters. Do it now. Before I get back home," he said.

"Yes, sir," said Miss Lilly.

"Your carriage is ready to go, sir." Harry had come into the kitchen. Master Hoover looked at him thoughtfully.

"That's fine. Wait for me outside," he replied.

He turned to Miss Lilly.

"Come with me," he ordered. She followed him to the library where Madam Charlotte and Emily were.

"Emily, go with Miss Lilly now. You'll be getting your things ready to move into the nanny's quarters." He didn't dare look into his wife's eyes.

"I'll be going into town for awhile. No need to wait up," he said to Madam Charlotte.

Madam Charlotte couldn't understand why he'd ruin Emily's party with his jealousy.

"I don't understand. What about Emily's party?"

∼

she asked. He just started walking away. She yelled, "Why are you so upset? Please don't walk out."

He turned to her and said, "The slaves around here will be treated like slaves from now on. They are not family." Then turned on his heels and walked out, interrupting a buzz of gossip that had erupted among the guests.

"The party is over, time to leave now," Master Hoover curtly said to his guests.

Shocked, everyone collected their belongings and left, except Percy Carson. He slipped onto the dark porch, where he hid himself from the Master. None of the other guests knew he was back there, not even the Madam, but I did.

Later on, rumors would fly and tongues would wag about that night. After everyone had gone, Madam Charlotte was alone. When she saw Percy, she was so pleased that he stayed. It was said that the guards saw something going on in the Master's bedroom window late that night, and they saw Percy Carson when he slipped away in the dark later on.

Master Hoover finally said something to Harry after he and I had climbed into the carriage. "Just drive around,"

Harry was worried about him, and asked, "What's wrong, Master?."

"I've got everything all worked out," said Master Hoover.

Even though I had a feeling about his plan, I was still surprised at what he said next.

≈

"Harry, you are not ever going to be with Emily in any way, except like a friend," he said and continued. "I've decided to take over the plantation the way my father taught me. Slaves on the Hoover Ranch don't act like slaves, and that's going to change as of now."

Harry was even more disappointed at what came next.

"Remember what my father said about you and me before he died?" He asked.

Harry didn't say a word, but Master Hoover kept on talking,

"I should learn to treat you like a slave, not a brother. Father said one day you would become my slave." Master looked Harry in the eye and said, "You a nigger, not a white man, you just remember that, *Old* Harry."

Harry, hurt by the new name his master was calling him when he was angry, but still didn't say a word, just kept on driving.

Master Hoover was still angry and then he said, "You aren't my friend or my brother. You disobey my orders; you'll be sold at the auction."

I sat there very surprised, just like Harry. Master Hoover began to act different when he realized that his feelings for Emily were real. He had changed when he saw that she had become a beautiful woman.

We rode around going nowhere in particular, listening to him talk to Harry about the new rules.

～

"Drive to the Montgomery Plantation, Old Harry," he finally ordered.

When we got there, the Montgomery family was just getting home from Emily's party themselves. I got out of the carriage with Master Hoover.

"Wait in the carriage," he ordered. Harry sat quietly; there was nothing else he could do.

I wanted to see what Master Hoover was going to do. I noticed that when Master Montgomery saw him coming to the door, he came out on the porch to meet him. Maybe neither one wanted any wives around. Master Hoover got started on his master plan, this was going to be an interesting night.

"I need another favor," Master Hoover began.

"You know, I was just thinking about you, because I am in need of a favor from you too," said Mr. Montgomery.

"Good. Here's the thing. I want Old Harry to stay out back with your slave woman tonight. I need to get rid of him from the big celebration. I need to work out my plan to get through to Emily easier."

"That's fine. Your boy can stay at my place for the night," replied Mr. Montgomery. "I want to go back to the Hoover Ranch with you tonight because I need a bed warmer. I've been looking at Miss Lilly, been wanting her for months." he said.

Master Hoover had to think about this.

"I want some of Miss Lilly real bad tonight," he said urgently.

His wife, Helen, was standing right at the door

and heard him telling Master Hoover that she was indisposed, as it was her monthly time, so he needed Miss Lilly.

Master Hoover was happy because his plan worked out. He headed back toward the carriage.

"Harry, I want you to help Master Montgomery with some work tomorrow." This was a lie. "You'll have to stay the night with Sweet Anna."

Harry wondered about the so-called wedding the next day, but Master Hoover settled that.

"Because of the celebration tomorrow, I won't be able to get you back on time." Harry knew this was part of the big master plan. There wasn't much he could do but just go along with it. Master Hoover didn't want Harry around until it was time for his next plan, when he would need the carriage.

"You come back tomorrow after the celebration. Wait 'till dark," he ordered.

Harry didn't ask any questions, he just got out of the carriage like Master Hoover told him to do, and walked toward the slave quarters to see Sweet Anna.

Master Montgomery was telling another version of plans to his wife. "Helen, I'm taking Edward home. He's going to leave his carriage here. I've got some work for his boy in the morning, so Harry will take the carriage home tomorrow night. I'll probably be late we are going for a drink with the fellows. No need to wait up."

They had told so many lies, I wondered if they even remembered them all. They got into the Montgomery carriage and headed toward the Hoover Ranch, laughing and talking about sex and women all the way. I got in the back of the carriage so I could hear them. They rode together so they could talk about the master plan and Emily, and that was what I wanted to hear.

"When I get back to the ranch, I plan to take Emily. I've got to win her confidence. I figure the best way is to make Harry look bad in her eyes," said Master Hoover.

I began to understand—he had it arranged all along. Now that Emily was out back in her new quarters, no one could stop him from getting to her. Master Hoover had waited for four long years to be able to touch Emily's body. Finally, he was going to carry out his master plan.

They pulled up in back of the house where Harry always parked the carriage. I watched them take the horses off the carriage and secure them in the barn, just like Harry did. Master Hoover took Mr. Montgomery to Miss Lilly's quarters.

"Where's Emily?" he said the moment she opened the door for him.

"Yes, sir, she's all moved into the nanny's quarters out back, just like you told me to do, Master." Then she saw Mr. Montgomery standing behind him and wondered what he wanted.

"You need anything else, Master?" she asked, hoping it wasn't what she was thinking.

"My friend, Mr. Montgomery, took a liking to

you and wants to visit with you for awhile," he said. She was very surprised at Master Hoover.

"Now Master Hoover, you know Willie Carson is my man, and you promised me a long time ago that you would never do this to me," she said. "Master, we are just finishing up supper," she added, hoping he'd go away. Master Hoover pushed his way into her quarters and Willie just sat on the floor eating.

"Sorry. Willie has to leave now." Before Miss Lilly could say another word, he continued. "If you like having Willie around the ranch, you had better get him out of here now, and be a real good girl to my friend here."

Miss Lilly didn't want to be there without Willie, so she asked him to leave.

"If you aren't good to Mr. Montgomery, you'll get a beating from both of us. And the next day, you'll find yourself at the auction," he said.

Miss Lilly right away told Willie to go to his quarters. Willie didn't speak a word; he got up from the floor and went to his quarters. Miss Lilly was very surprised because Master Hoover had never done anything like this to her. When Miss Lilly was alone with Mr. Montgomery, who was a big man, he picked up her petite, half-white body and laid her on the padding and blankets she used for a bed on the floor, which she had already made up for Willie. Mr. Montgomery couldn't wait. He started touching and kissing her breasts, then taking off her clothes. Miss Lilly didn't try to stop him; she let him have his

~

way with her like a good girl, just as Master Hoover said. Mr. Montgomery seemed to have wanted her badly; he finished quickly. Miss Lilly was glad of that. She wanted it to be over, and when it was, she thought he would leave, but he didn't.

"I tell you, girl, you sure have some good stuff," he said, then turned over, fell asleep, and began snoring.

Miss Lilly looked at him and tried to move his arms away from around her neck. He had gone to sleep holding her in his arms and I watched her trying to get loose. Every time she started to move that old goat would open his eyes. She had to stay there until he woke up, and she didn't get to see Willie any more that night. I really wanted to help her, but I couldn't.

I was surprised when I turned to leave, and I caught Master Hoover watching them too, looking through the window. When Master Hoover left Miss Lilly's, he went straight to Emily's quarters and knocked on her door. I ran to catch up with him because I did not want to miss anything. When Emily opened the door she seemed surprised to see him. Emily had on her nightgown made of thin soft white cotton material. She looked like she was looking for someone to come by.

It's late and something must have happened, Emily's face read.

She was wondering why she hadn't heard Harry bring the carriage back. She had gone to bed and was almost asleep. When she had heard the light knock on her door, she had jumped up to answer it.

∾

"Oh my, Master Hoover, are you still angry?" she said when she realized it was Master Hoover. Master Hoover stepped into her quarters, put his arm around Emily, and walked with her toward her bed, making her sit down.

"No, Emily. I'm not angry anymore. I wasn't angry with you anyway."

"But Master, who made you so angry?"

"I was angry with Old Harry. He is not doing what is expected of him around here. We had planned for him to be your husband, but he doesn't seem to be happy about it."

"What did he do?" she asked.

Master Hoover was not listening to her, because he was caught up with her beauty. He found himself sitting just looking into her eyes and wanting her so badly. He couldn't help himself; he took her into his arms and kissed her gently. Emily was confused by his actions and wasn't sure what to do. Then Master Hoover stopped kissing her and acted like something was wrong.

"I have something to tell you before tomorrow," he said.

I was on my way outside, but I heard him talking about what was supposed to be her wedding day, so I decided to stay. She looked into his eyes for answers.

"Did something happen to Harry?" she asked.

"Old Harry is all right, but he doesn't want to marry you."

≈

Emily seemed sad at first, and then angry. "Does Harry have another lady that he wants to marry?" she asked.

Master Hoover was happy to hear her ask that question.

"It appears so. Harry has a field slave named Sweet Anna that he has been seeing for years, who lives on Mr. Montgomery's place," he replied.

Now after listening to everyone, I knew that was not entirely the truth because the slave men around town used Sweet Anna only if Master Montgomery allowed it. The white men used her for a bed warmer whenever Master Montgomery wanted to give her to them. Sweet Anna was a beautiful woman, and all the white men called her a "high yellow nigger." They all loved having sex with her, and Harry was no exception.

Knowing all this, Master Hoover went on explaining his version of things to Emily. "Old Harry took me to a business meeting at the Montgomery place tonight, and then he went to see Sweet Anna. When I got ready to come home, I found Old Harry in bed with her—that's when he told me how he felt about you. He said he didn't want any woman but Sweet Anna. Then he wanted to know if he had to marry you, even though he didn't want to."

Master Hoover was really making up lies just to get on the good side of Emily. "Old Harry asked me to tell you that he was not interested in marrying you; he's in love with Sweet Anna." He embellished these lies with several more details, then went on to say, "I'm very angry with Old Harry, and I have decided to sell him at the slave auction tomorrow."

"Please, don't sell Harry because I'm not interested in marrying any man if he doesn't want me. No one should be punished for wanting to be with the person they love," said Emily.

Master Hoover felt the same should apply to him; he didn't think he should be punished for loving and wanting to be with her. He sat there thinking that he wanted to be married to her, but he knew that wasn't possible.

"Well, Old Harry wanted to stay the night with Sweet Anna, and I'm going to send him away," said Master Hoover. He stood up. Emily jumped up in dismay.

"Oh no, Master Hoover, please don't send him away. I just don't want a man that doesn't want me," said Emily, with tears filling her eyes.

This pleased Master Hoover. He never wanted to send Harry away anyway, but he wanted Emily to think he was protecting her.

They stood looking at each other, their eyes filled with emotion. Emily had been prepared to become a wife and a mother for four years, and she wanted to make love. She always wanted to make passionate love to the man intended for her. Madam Charlotte had told her to enjoy having sex while trying to conceive her children.

Emily had been looking forward to using on Harry some of the techniques that she had in her heart and mind from her book. She remembered the book had drawings of lovemaking. I was fascinated with the knowledge that she had obtained about being sexy and making love. Emily was ready to use it on her man; she just never thought that her man would be Master Hoover.

"What should I tell Madam Charlotte?" Emily asked. She seemed more worried about hurting Madam Charlotte than she was about Harry.

"We're not going to tell Madam Charlotte anything. Just let her think you're getting married to Harry," he said.

This was part of his master plan.

"Madam Charlotte wants to have a baby by the end of the year," Master Hoover explained, going on to the next step of his plan. "That means you'll need to be impregnated right away in order to be ready to breastfeed Madam's baby. I'll father your first child, but you must never tell Madam Charlotte, or anyone else for that matter. This will be our secret."

"Madam Charlotte has been good to me, and I don't want to disappoint her," said Emily.

Master Hoover knew in his heart that he had to convince Emily that it was all right to father her child; he also had to arrange it so that absolutely no one could be told about it. Master Hoover was proud of his ability to manipulate and privately called himself "The Master of Deceit."

"But Master, what if I am asked who the father of my child is? What should I say?" Emily asked.

"Tell them it is your husband Harry's child. He is the only slave on this place that looks white; this will protect Madam Charlotte's feelings." He said.

Madam Charlotte had taught Emily how to keep her body clean, how to read, and all about men so she would be ready to become a woman in her own home someday. Now the time had come, Emily was actually going to use the knowledge that she had learned with a man for the first time.

Master Hoover had told Emily that Harry was in on their secret, which was a lie. Master Hoover knew that he would need to tell Madam Charlotte that Emily and Harry were married so he planned to go ahead with the fake wedding with Harry, and Madam Charlotte didn't realize that Harry wouldn't even be there. Master Hoover had been dying to get to Emily and he couldn't wait any longer. He had it all planned.

They looked at each other, each struggling with rising feelings of need. He pulled her to the floor, where he covered her with kisses. As he kissed her and touched her, he made love to her, holding her and experiencing her for the first time. They couldn't keep their eyes from each other as the passion between them burned.

It was refreshing to me to see how passionate they were toward each other, but it seemed to be over as soon as it got started. Suddenly, Emily's face looked worried about something.

"What's wrong?" asked Master Hoover and she answered,

"It seems wrong somehow, the way I feel in my heart for you, but I can't stop myself from wanting more of you."

He was happy to hear her say that because he knew that he wanted more of her too.

"I don't like lying to my Madam like this because we have never lied to each other before," Emily said, worried. She paused for a moment and continued. "I love Madam Charlotte because she took me in, and raised me as her own daughter, and taught me everything I know."

"This isn't wrong, because we love each other, as long as Madam Charlotte doesn't know, everything will be fine." He replied gently.

Emily seemed unsure, so the Master added more deceit.

"Emily, if you don't do this for Madam, she will never be able to have a child of her own. You must understand that Madam needs you to have my baby. She can't relax about having a child of her own unless she thinks you are having a child, but Old Harry doesn't want you."

"That's true," she said.

Well, he had convinced her to have his child, and she started to smile. I didn't want to leave the room, even though I thought that I should, but I loved watching them make love. After all, I was sent there just to watch. I watched her pull him close, kissing his lips then touching all over him to show her feelings for him as they made love again. This time Emily was not sad after making love to him; she thought everything was great the second time around.

"We aren't hurting anyone if we keep it a secret," she whispered.

I thought, *My goodness, he is teaching her how to be as deceitful as himself!*

"You are absolutely right," said Master Hoover. "Everything works out for everyone this way." He held her in his arms. "I promise that I'll always look out for you and our children," he said.

As I stood there watching and listening to them, I knew without a doubt that they were in love with each other. That wasn't hard to figure out. I could tell by the way they looked at each other and by the way they made love to each other. I always believed that Emily had fallen in love with Master Hoover from the beginning.

He was a very appealing man, tall and thin, with light blue eyes, brown hair, nice teeth. And he was romantic.

This is my way of thanking him for being so kind, Emily's face showed her thoughts, *and getting pregnant will be my gift to Madam Charlotte.* After convincing herself that they were doing the right thing, and making love to complete satisfaction, Emily was happy. I think that she loved making love to Master Hoover as much as he loved making love to her.

After they finished, it was late and Master Hoover

prepared to leave Emily. He had to arrange the big secret that he was planning for Emily the next day. His master plan wasn't complete yet.

Emily was excited about the big celebration ahead of her, come morning. By now she knew it was a celebration instead of her wedding. She thought of it as celebrating her love for Master Hoover. Only Madam Charlotte thought it was Emily's wedding day.

"Have you ever had sex with anyone before me?" asked Master Hoover before he left.

"Once, my father, who was my mother's master, took me," she said.

Master Hoover was surprised because she had been just a girl when he bought her.

"How old were you?" he asked.

"I was only ten years old. It was painful," she said.

She smiled at him and said, "But it was not painful with you, Master. It was wonderful."

"But how did you know just what to do?"

"Madam Charlotte taught me everything I know about life."

This made him wonder about Madam "Did she teach her how to make love?" he wondered.

It was very late when Master Hoover got dressed to leave and kissed Emily goodnight. Just as he left Emily's quarters, he saw Master Montgomery leaving Miss Lilly's quarters, getting into his horse carriage.

Montgomery must have had a good time with Miss

Lilly, the way he was smiling, thought Mr. Hoover. It was late when he arrived inside the big house. It was three in the morning, and Madam Charlotte was asleep. Master Hoover was relieved because he was tired and had to get some rest for Emily's so-called wedding, which was to take place in a few hours. Master Hoover would run the show. He wanted to be well-rested for another night like the one he'd just had with Emily.

CHAPTER 3

Morning came quickly, and it was time to prepare for Emily's so-called wedding. It was set for noon and it was already nine in the morning.

Madam Charlotte felt a little guilty about the night before, so she turned over in bed to kiss her husband, but he was still asleep. That didn't stop her from reaching down under the sheets and touching him. Master Hoover must have been dreaming about Emily, which broadened the smile on his face while Madam Charlotte caressed him. Seeing him smiling like that, it seemed to make her ready for him.

This had never happened this way in storytelling with my Big Daddy. Master Hoover and Madam Charlotte were not in love when they got married; their parents put them together, so the story goes. Master Hoover must have been half sleep and thinking about Emily when he was making love to Madam. She continued to touch him and they made love.

"Oh Emily, it's so good," he called out, enjoying the feeling. He started kissing Madam Charlotte, as though he was dreaming of making love to Emily. Powerfully aroused, he put his arms around his wife, turned over, and continued to make passionate love to her. "Oh! Baby," he groaned, still asleep.

When he kissed his wife she said, "What's come over you, we have never kissed this way before?" He still laid asleep in her arms with a relaxing face.

When he awakened he looked for Emily—and came face to face with his wife, who was lying under his body. *My master plan is all over now*, he thought. He didn't know what to do or say.

Madam Charlotte was feeling really good, never mind that he had called her "Emily." There she was, smiling at him.

I was dreaming of making love to Emily, but it turned out to be a nightmare, he thought.

"What did I say to you while we were making love, dear?" he asked sheepishly.

"You said good things to me, things I've never heard you say before," she replied.

"I thought you were trying to apologize to me for the way you acted at Emily's party."

When they got out of bed that Saturday morning, it was after eleven in the morning, and Emily's so-called wedding was to take place at noon.

Sometimes Master Hoover would give the slaves free time when there was a special occasion, like Emily's wedding, and he had set up this event on his plantation for only his slaves to attend. Though he said the celebration was only for slaves, he intended to be there. Madam Charlotte still wanted to attend this wedding.

"She's like my daughter, and I should be by her side on her wedding day," said Madam Charlotte. It was obvious that Master Hoover was not happy about the whole idea of her going to the slave quarters and interfering with his plans.

"You are not going to attend Emily's affair—you aren't allowed to attend any slave affair, even if it is for your daughter," he said. He reminded her of the white man's law in the South. "White women are not allowed to socialize with the slaves." That had been the white man's rule for many years. "And by the way," he said. "I meant what I said about making some changes around here, Madam. From now on, slaves will be treated like slaves."

Master Hoover knew Madam Charlotte would be hurt if he did not allow her to attend Emily's affair, especially with her thinking it was Emily's wedding day.

"I've decided to do something special for you and Emily after the celebration," he offered. "I was going to surprise you, but I'll tell you now: I've got a picture man coming. You will be able to see the whole wedding in pictures! It will be like you were there the whole time." He knew he was scoring points with Madam Charlotte, so he continued. "Also, I'm going to take you both into town to shop, and you can buy Emily some of those cute little nightgowns. After all, she'll be a new bride." Boy that made

Madam Charlotte happy, since she thought that the sexy nightgowns were for Harry's eyes.

Harry, Emily, Miss Lilly, and Willie had all been told different stories, but Master Hoover was sure no one would put all the facts together. He gave Miss Lilly a story because she had to play along when she came into the big house to get the food.

When Madam Charlotte saw Miss Lilly come into the house, she ran into the room after her. She couldn't wait to hear some news.

"How is she feeling? How does she look?" she asked eagerly. Miss Lilly knew that she had to keep everything in order with the master plan. She had to lie.

"Harry and Emily look very happy, and they look just fine as can be," Miss Lilly told Madam Charlotte. Miss Lilly knew how much Madam Charlotte cared for Emily, and that she was hurting since she couldn't attend the so-called wedding. So she went along with Master Hoover and said things to make her feel better.

"Emily looks real pretty, Madam, you have made a proper lady of her," she said.

The lies were going pretty well, so Miss Lilly decided to decorate them a bit more, "Madam Charlotte, because of you Emily was looking like a queen today, and they were just the best looking couple this side of the Mississippi!"

"Oh! Miss Lilly, you are an angel from up above! I really needed to know something."

Madam Charlotte felt much better, thanks to Miss

Lilly, but it didn't stop there. Miss Lilly was feeling good about herself, so she started adding even more information to her story.

"Madam Charlotte, you should see the way Harry kissed Emily, and she held him very close, it was so romantic." Miss Lilly was enjoying herself, trying to help Madam Charlotte feel better.

Just as she was getting ready to make up a few more things, Master Hoover walked in. He had been listening to Miss Lilly's lies behind the door the whole time, wanting to see what she would say to Madam Charlotte when he wasn't around. When Miss Lilly told the lie about the kissing, he put a stop to it. He didn't enjoy thinking about Emily kissing anyone else, and he was afraid Miss Lilly might soon say the wrong thing. *No one is as good at deceiving people as me,* he thought.

"Now Miss Lilly, let's not gossip, that's enough details for Madam." He went on to say,

"You get back out there and keep your big eyes open." Miss Lilly stopped talking and ran out back as fast as she could.

He's gonna get me for talking too much, she thought. But he wasn't angry with her. In fact, he was proud of the way Miss Lilly had handled herself.

"Just don't talk so much next time, the trick is, only tell as little as possible," he told her later.

Dressed in his best suit, Master Hoover attended the entire affair, watching Emily all afternoon and looking like he wanted to marry Emily himself.

~

Emily wore the beautiful wedding dress that Madam Charlotte bought for her for this occasion.

Wanting to make sure that this day was remembered forever, Master Hoover ordered a picture man to take photographs of Emily's wedding day and all the slaves. These pictures were for him, but he also thought they would fool Madam Charlotte. He told Madam Charlotte that she could put one on the wall in the big house, which pleased her very much, because she had wanted to see Emily in her wedding dress badly. He kept his word and had a large picture framed of Emily and mounted in the foyer. When Madam Charlotte wasn't around, he'd study that picture and think private thoughts.

Master Hoover even took a picture of himself with Emily at the wedding, as if he were the groom. Later he gave that picture to Emily, and until her death, no one ever saw that picture except Emily and Master Hoover. Emily kept it hidden in her private box in the nanny's quarters. She looked at it whenever she felt alone. On her deathbed, she gave the picture to her seventh son, but by then Master Hoover was long gone.

One thing Master Hoover didn't do was let the picture man take pictures of Harry alone with Emily. Harry wasn't invited to the celebration at all, but he had been ordered to show up later to drive the carriage to the river. Master Hoover kept the picture man waiting until Harry arrived after the celebration, and ordered a photograph taken of Harry with

Sister Harriet, Pastor Martin, Willie, Miss Lilly, and himself. And of course, Emily.

In his master plan, Master Hoover intended to honeymoon with Emily by the river, where they would make love under the moonlight. Emily was expecting a passionate night celebrating their beginning. She felt proud because when Madam Charlotte had taken her to town to pick out her wedding dress she had also bought Emily a soft white dress to wear on the special first night with her husband.

"This is for Harry's eyes only," Madam Charlotte had whispered, because the gown was completely sheer.

"Don't wear a thing under this dress, to show off your body. That will arouse Harry's nature," she also said in a whisper.

Emily planned to wear that dress with Master Hoover to arouse him, because he was her secret lover. Master Hoover had told Madam Charlotte a lie; he was going to drive the wedding couple to the river for their honeymoon, and wouldn't be back until late that night.

When Harry arrived back at Hoover Ranch with the carriage, he hoped to get some sleep before he was asked to do anything because he was very tired. He had been working for Mr. Montgomery the whole day. The moment he got to the ranch, Master Hoover handed him a suit and told him to put it on just for show. He told him to hurry so they could take pictures with Emily, Willie, Miss Lilly and himself, before the picture man left. The pictures were finally finished.

"Okay, get to your quarters for some rest. Be ready to go in one hour," said Master Hoover, finally.

Harry headed toward his quarters by the barn, very much in need of sleep because he had spent the night with Sweet Anna. It seemed like a short hour when Master Hoover showed up at the barn to wake Harry, pretending that he was planning to chauffeur the newlyweds. His master plan was working from start to finish, and he was pleased.

Well, all these manipulations were just too much for me, but I had made up my mind to stay out of the way. I kept telling myself that I was there just to watch. I decided to go with Master Hoover to the river to see him make love to Emily again. I wanted to see the passionate love affair that was getting ready to make history, because I sensed that somehow it was my own history as well as theirs.

Master Hoover knew that Madam Charlotte would be watching in the window as they left. After Master Hoover got Harry out of bed and ready to go, Emily came out looking sexy in her soft white dress. Besides the sheer dress, she had on only a beautiful wrap around her shoulders.

I noticed that Harry still looked sleepy, but when he took one look at Emily, it sure woke him up. As they drove past Madam Charlotte's window, she was indeed watching, just as Master Hoover thought. Madam Charlotte saw Emily and Harry riding inside the carriage looking like newlyweds and Master Hoover driving the horses.

"Wave to her and smile, now," he ordered the so-called honeymooners. Master Hoover made sure that Emily knew that she was not allowed to talk to Harry at any time.

"Don't embarrass him. He won't know what to do if you mention what I told you about his love affair with Sweet Anna," he advised her.

"Master, I am not going to talk to him about anything because it is embarrassing to me too, seeing that he preferred another woman over me. Why should I talk to him anyway? I'm not promised to him anymore," Emily said emphatically.

Master Hoover was proud of her and impressed. The master plan was still working.

Master Hoover drove his carriage away from the ranch until he thought he was far enough away, then he stopped and told Harry to get out and finish driving them to the river. Emily never looked at Harry, nor did she speak to him.

Madam Charlotte knew they would be gone late into the next morning. They didn't know it, but as soon as they passed out of view another carriage was coming down the road toward the Hoover Ranch. It was Percy Carson, on his way to visit Madam Charlotte. The masters of the Montgomery and Carson plantations were never stopped at any time, day or night. They were always welcome at each other's homes, without question.

Madam Charlotte knew it was going to be a long evening all alone. So, she had sent Willie to Percy Carson with a message inviting him to come calling that night. She\was also working on her own Master Plan, which involved increasing the amount of passionate love in her life.

When Madam Charlotte saw the carriage coming toward the house she ran down the stairs, out the door, onto the porch and into Percy Carson's arms. They kissed, hugged, and went into the house, straight to the master bedroom.

Percy Carson had fallen in love with her as a young boy and had never stopped loving her. Tenderly, passionately, they made love to each other for the second time.

Master Hoover and Emily were locked in tender conversation.

"I just don't feel comfortable about Old Harry now that he disrespected you," he said.

"I'll admit that I was very angry with Harry for not wanting to marry me," Emily admitted. "Sometimes I really want to make him sorry about his choice to be with Sweet Anna."

I do believe Emily was jealous, and she really

believed Master Hoover had told her the truth about Harry. She didn't know that he had lied to her just like he lied to everyone else, and she didn't realize he prided himself on being "The Master of Deceit." Master Hoover put his arms around her, and they began kissing and holding each other. Emily was hoping that Harry was looking, and he was, until he was told to drive on.

Harry was surprised at the way Emily acted toward him. For my part, I really wanted to do something, but I decided not to try to interfere anymore.

I'm just here to watch, I kept telling myself.

When Harry got to the river, he stopped the carriage. "What a beautiful moonlight tonight," he commented.

Master Hoover just looked at him. "You just stay here in the carriage and get some sleep. You're sleepy."

Then he took Emily by the hand, and helped her out of the carriage with tender care. Putting his arm around her body, he walked her out closer to the river. They found a spot around the bend behind a large rock very near the river. It had a small waterfall. I could tell Master Hoover was trying to find a place far out of Harry's vision.

Safely out of sight, they felt comfortable being romantic with each other. Their honeymoon spot was covered with soft green grass. Master Hoover carried the same blanket that he used to wrap around Emily the night he brought her to the ranch from the slave auction.

≈

Harry was so angry with Master Hoover that he was tempted to tell Emily what the Master had done to stop their marriage. He wanted her to know about the master plan. He thought Master Hoover was trying to have his cake and eat it too. But he knew there wasn't anything that he could do, so Harry just resigned himself to losing Emily, who had never been intended for him anyway.

Master Hoover took the blanket and spread it over that soft green grass. As he put down the blanket, Emily slipped her arms around him. She began to touch him all over. Master Hoover was surprised, but thrilled that she was so relaxed and ready to make love. The moon danced over their heads as they touched each other and rolled all over the beautiful soft grass carpet. They were filled with passionate desire as they wrapped their bodies around each other, kissing each other with deep emotions. They made love under the moonlight.

"Oh, you're marvelous," he said. He was still amazed at her knowledge of tenderness. He loved the way she turned on that burning desire in him, an intensity that he had never known before. Master Hoover held her in his arms after they made love and looked into her eyes filled with love.

"This is a romantic evening that belongs only to us," he whispered, nuzzling Emily's ear.

To my surprise, a different voice whispered to me. "This was Mama Emily."

The slave my Big Daddy told me about as we sat on

the porch in Mississippi when I was a child. I am a descendant of this night of passion by the river, I realized.

Then I heard Mama Emily speak. "Master, I would have made Harry a good wife. I would have given him my soul.

"You can forget Old Harry. He belongs to Sweet Anna. You belong to me now, and I want you give me your soul," he said, adding, "I have loved you from the start."

I watched them kiss again, passionately making love all over again. Before they left the river, Emily looked into his eyes and said, "I love you."

"I love you too, and I love making love to you with all of my heart," he replied.

Master Hoover knew then that he had convinced Emily that it was all right to be lovers. At this point Emily was enjoying intimacy with him. The secret of it all made it more desirable to her, and nothing else mattered. Sex was new to Emily, and she was really enjoying it and wanted him whenever he wanted her.

"Don't tell Old Harry anything we talked about," Master Hoover reminded her. "Our love is our secret only. We want Madam Charlotte to think Old Harry fathered your baby." In his heart, he really wanted Emily to be his wife, but he realized that was not possible.

Emily knew that she was hooked on Master Hoover and it looked like he was even more hooked on her. I began to wonder if Emily would ever learn the truth about Master Hoover. Somehow I didn't

∼

think Emily wanted to know, or maybe she already knew and didn't care. I noticed them getting ready to leave the river, so I picked myself up from my spot and ran to get in the carriage before anyone else.

I had forgotten that Harry was in the carriage sleeping. When I got in the carriage he got up, as though he heard me. They all returned home about three in the morning and by this time, Master Hoover was very sleepy.

"Carry Emily back to her room, Old Harry, and don't wake her up," he said.

Master Hoover looked up at the window to see if Madam Charlotte was still up. He hoped not, but he was surprised because she stood at the window, looking out. Master Hoover feared that he'd been found out. He never suspected that Percy Carson had just left and that was the reason Madam Charlotte was still up. She had just finished cleaning herself up in a bath and she was hoping that Master Hoover would be too sleepy to want sex from her. She was trying to think of a plan that would keep him from wanting her.

He's had a long day, she thought. But he'd been watching Harry and Emily make love, and was sure to come in wanting her. Madam Charlotte was distracted for a minute when she saw Harry carrying Emily. *How romantic,* she thought. *Oh! I'd better get in bed!* She hurried to her bed and climbed in, pretending she was asleep.

She didn't know that Master Hoover saw her in the window, so she didn't know that he knew she was still up. Master Hoover was wishing she was asleep because he didn't want to make love to her either. So Master Hoover decided to think of something to do for awhile, hoping she'd go to sleep before he made it to the room.

I guess I'll go with Old Harry, he decided. He probably needs help getting her inside. So he accompanied Harry until Emily was settled in, and then sent him back to put the horses away.

"See to the horses, and then get back to the barn for bed," Master Hoover instructed. Harry was mighty angry at Master Hoover for taking beautiful Emily from him, but what could he do?

When Master Hoover got to his bedroom, he was surprised and pleased to find his wife asleep. I could tell she was pretending. She knew that he would smell her body, fresh from bathing after being with Percy. When he got into the bed, she turned over to kiss him. Then she opened her legs all across the bed in a sexy way to let him know that she was ready for him.

"I've been waiting for you, sweetheart," she said.

"I'm awfully tired. It was a real long day, with Emily's wedding and all," he said.

Madam Charlotte was happy to hear him say that, but she didn't want him to know she was glad.

"I understand," she said while thinking, *This*

is going great. "I'll wait until you feel better. Good night, sweetheart." And with that she turned to go to sleep. With a surprised look on his face, he turned over and went to sleep right away. I was surprised too. I watched Madam Charlotte and she seemed happy and content. They were both working their own master plans.

CHAPTER 4

I was beginning to feel very tired and sleepy, but I hadn't been sleepy or even felt tired like this before. Then I heard someone call out my name. I went to the window, but I couldn't see anyone there. Then I heard it again. It was louder this time, and it kept getting louder and louder. I could hear it very clearly.

"Tyara," it said, and it sounded far away. I wondered if I was being sent to another place. Then I heard it again as if they were yelling for me. "T...y...a...r...a..." It was getting closer and closer to me.

"Open your eyes," the voice said, but I thought my eyes were already open. I started to think I was dreaming, but when I opened my eyes, everything was clear to me. I was sitting at my desk in front of my computer. I knew then that I had been on a trip with a spirit. When I looked at my computer screen, I noticed that I had been writing down everything as I saw it. I was very frightened. I had written many pages of my imaginary story about slave times, but I didn't remember writing it. I could only remember the trip back in time; it was so fantastic that I could hardly wait to return. I felt the spirit all around me in the room, until I heard voices talking in the house downstairs.

The first thoughts I had were that more spirits were downstairs. Then I remembered my brother and my best friend were visiting. To me it was more like they were visiting with each other because I was upstairs writing my dream story, and they were downstairs talking.

I jumped up from the computer and ran downstairs to tell them about my dream, but it didn't seem like a dream.

"Girl, you look like you saw a ghost!" my girlfriend was concerned about me when she saw me. I told her about the spirits.

"You better stop writing for awhile, before you get sick. You are getting too fascinated with the spirits," she said.

It was too fascinating for me to stop. I had written everything down on the computer and I knew that I had to see it through and finish.

I went upstairs and started to read what I had written, and in no time I was on my journey again. I wasn't asleep, but the spirit was inside me again.

I listened carefully to the voice in my head, which sounded like my Big Daddy, but I couldn't see him. So I sat down in the chair in Master Hoover's bedroom and watched Master Hoover and Madam

Charlotte sleeping in their bed. Sitting there in the chair, I fell asleep too.

When I opened my eyes, I felt the presence of my Big Daddy standing over me. I knew he was there to comfort and encourage me not to quit searching for my past. I could feel him and hear him in my heart, but I couldn't see him. I started to wonder if I was really dreaming, at least I thought I was, and my eyes started to close again. As my eyes closed, the voice was trying to tell me something but I couldn't hear it. I had a sense that time was passing very quickly.

When I opened my eyes I was still in Master Hoover's bedroom, but the Hoovers were no longer in bed. Then I realized that it was not the same.

The room looked new. It was set up for a baby. Even the chair was different, and I woke up in what looked like a handmade white chair trimmed in oak wood, designed to recline back. I was in a baby's room set up for two babies. I wanted to know who was about to give birth.

Lots of baby things were in this room. I noticed there were two baby beds. *Someone must be having twins*, I thought. I tried to figure out who it would be.

I heard voices in the hallway coming toward the room. I was frightened so I ran behind the chair, but soon I realized that they couldn't see me anyway, so I came out from behind the chair and stood there.

It was Madam Charlotte and Emily.

Oh my goodness, they are both very pregnant. But I wasn't gone that long.

～

This must be like watching a movie; if you don't stay awake you miss a lot. Boy, I really missed a lot, but I was so happy that I hadn't gone for good, because I really wanted to see Emily have her firstborn son, who I knew would be my great-great-grandfather.

When they came into the room they were both talking about the babies' room. Master Hoover was building a new part to his master bedroom for the babies.

Now I understand why the room looks different. It is being turned into a nursery for the babies.

They looked like they were ready to give birth any day now. I wanted to talk to them, so I tried. "When are the babies due to arrive?" I asked.

They kept on talking as though they didn't hear me, but to my surprise Emily stopped and looked around as though she heard something.

"What's wrong, Emily?" asked Madam Charlotte.

"I thought I heard someone talking to us," said Emily.

"I didn't hear anything, what did the voice say?" asked Madam Charlotte.

"It sounded like a little girl's voice, and the little girl asked when our babies are due," Emily replied.

Then they laughed, because they had been talking about names for a girl child, but they knew that most men wanted boys.

"Harry wants a boy," said Emily.

At first, I was confused when she said that, then I thought, *Oh, I see, Emily is still playing that game with Madam Charlotte. She is keeping the secret about who the child's father really was. Maybe Madam Charlotte's child's real father was also a secret.*

Emily wanted a boy, but she didn't want Madam Charlotte to know that she wanted a lot of children, and all boys. She was afraid of having girls. She feared that they would take the girls away from her, or they would use her as bed warmers for some other slave owner. Emily had been taken away from her own mother and didn't want that to happen to her child.

I heard them say the babies were due in a month. I thought to myself, *If that is true, it would mean a little over half a year had passed already!*

I couldn't believe it. I'd only taken a nap for a few minutes. Well, I wasn't about to take any more naps because I didn't want to miss any more, not when babies were about to be born!

"I hear Master Hoover coming, Madam. He is home from his business trip," said Emily.

"We must get ready for dinner. It must be time if he's home. Let's go check with Miss Lilly," said Madam Charlotte.

They left the room and walked right into Master Hoover. I noticed that one thing had not changed at all—the way Master Hoover looked at Emily, even pregnant. She looked at him with passion also. She was eight months pregnant with her first child, and looked as though it was time to give birth any day.

Madam Charlotte looked even bigger. It looked to be a large baby.

~

"Miss Lilly's calling for dinner," Master Hoover said.

I ran out into the kitchen to see her and saw that she was having a baby also. She was as big as the others were. *There will be lots of children running around this place soon*, I said to myself. They were all going to give birth around the same time.

I noticed how Madam Charlotte looked at Master Hoover when he entered the room; she was watching him as he looked at Emily. Madam Charlotte reached out and hugged Master Hoover. I knew that she was just showing off in front of Emily. Madam Charlotte noticed her husband's reluctance to hug her.

"Don't be shy in front of Emily," she said. She was noticing something.

However, all of her passionate looks at Master Hoover were just for show, because Madam Charlotte was still in love with Percy. He had tried to get her to leave her husband and move to Chicago with him.

"Oh, Percy, I can't leave my family here in Mississippi," she had said.

She also knew that she was often ill and was unable to take care of a baby without Emily's help. Madam Charlotte would need to take Emily with her if she left, but Emily would never leave Master Hoover anyway.

Well, Percy Carson loved her a lot because he

changed his mind about Chicago and stayed in Mississippi, just to be near her.

"I've lived most of my life without you already, and now that we have found each other again, I'm not about to let you go. I'll take you any way that I can get you, even if it has to be a secret forever!" he said.

Emily had moved into the nanny's quarters inside the big house, since she was going to start breast-feeding the babies as soon as they were born. Madam Charlotte and Emily acted just like mother and daughter. They were having fun going over baby things and getting ready for their little bundles of joy to arrive.

Later that night, Emily took her very first walk around the ranch alone. After she had her dinner alone in the nanny's quarters, she felt depressed. She left the big house and went for a walk around the ranch. Although Emily was supposed to be part of the family, at times she did eat her dinner alone in her room.

Sometimes Master Hoover would go to keep her company for a while and they would make love. This night he didn't, so she went for a walk. Madam Charlotte looked out the window and saw her walking around the ranch alone. She called Master Hoover.

"Where is Old Harry? I don't want Emily walking around this big ranch alone at night, not in her condition."

"I'll go look for him," said Master Hoover.

He knew that Harry was no longer around Hoover Ranch because he'd gotten rid of him. Master Hoover didn't really trust him around Emily.

He had traded Harry to Master Montgomery for a favor, but Madam Charlotte still didn't know about it. Now Harry could only come to Hoover Ranch to make deliveries. Madam Charlotte saw him coming and going and kept believing he fathered Emily's baby. I was amazed at the way Master Hoover controlled people's lives.

Sweet Anna and Harry were falling in love since they were together all the time. They had a child on the way, and since he was there most of the time, he decided to act like he was Sweet Anna's husband. She loved him too.

Master Hoover left the house quickly to go see about Emily. When he caught up with her, she was surprised to see him. He wanted to kiss her badly, but knew Madam Charlotte was watching from the window; he also knew that she couldn't hear what they were saying to each other so they talked.

Trying to convince Madam that he was talking to Emily about how unsafe it was for her to be walking alone in her condition with his hand gestures, "I want to take you in my arms and hold you forever, but Madam is watching, so we have to find another moment."

To Madam Charlotte, it seemed that they were

talking about Harry. She'd been afraid that Emily might get hurt walking alone during this time in her pregnancy, especially at night. Reassured to see Master Hoover walking with her now, she turned and walked away from the window.

I went along with Master Hoover and Emily as they walked. I didn't want to miss anything in their relationship.

"I've missed you terribly since moving into the main nanny's quarters, we can't see each other anymore, not until Madam Charlotte and I have the babies." Emily said with a sad look on her face.

"I know, I miss you too, but we haven't been together since you moved inside the big house," said Master Hoover. Emily missed him, and he missed her.

"Neither of us likes the separation, but there's nothing we can do about it," said Emily.

As Master Hoover walked with Emily, he started thinking about the way that Madam Charlotte came into his life, and felt this was a good time to talk to Emily about his life.

Emily noticed him in deep thought and asked, "What's on your mind?"

"I was just thinking about times when I was younger," he said.

"Tell me," she urged.

"Well I met this girl when I was away at boarding

school in Chicago. She was the most beautiful girl that I had ever seen, and I fell in love with her and wanted to marry her, but she was not a white girl. She was one-third colored. She looked white, but she never denied the fact that she was colored." He stopped walking and looked at Emily. "You remind me a lot of that girl, and how much I once loved her."

"What happened? Why didn't you marry her?" asked Emily.

"I asked her to marry me," he answered and continued, "I wanted her to tell my father that she was a white girl so we could be married, but she wouldn't tell a lie about who she really was, even for me."

He choked up suddenly at the memory of losing his first love. Emily noticed the tears that were rolling down his face.

He went on, "Emily, she said to me, 'I wouldn't tell a lie like that to anyone!' And after that I felt her slip away from me like running water."

"Why didn't you just tell the truth?" asked Emily.

"Well, she had a light-skinned colored mother and a white father. She was beautiful inside and outside, just like you, Emily. So I did tell the truth. I went back home and told my father that I wanted to marry her."

"Good for you," said Emily.

"But my father said she was just a nigger and he wasn't about to have any nigger blood running through the veins of the Hoover family. Emily, that's why I've never really approved of slavery and the reason I protect my slaves today. I never have condoned slavery—this was handed to me from my father." He added, "A man should be free, and one day, Emily, that will be so."

"How did you meet Madam Charlotte?" Emily asked, changing the subject.

"My father was paid a large sum of money to arrange my marriage with Charlotte Montgomery," said Master Hoover, and continued, "She was my best friend at the time. Our parents were friends, so we spent every Sunday in each other's company."

Master Hoover looked so sad telling this story to Emily, but I felt as though he needed to tell her to clear his own mind. Somehow, I knew he felt it would put his heart at peace.

"One evening, father brought Charlotte home. 'This here's your wife, boy!' he said. The dowry had already been paid. I had no choice in the matter it was marry her or lose my inheritance." He looked into Emily's eyes. "So you see, Emily, I was never in love with Charlotte for a wife. Our marriage was arranged by our parents. Charlotte and I were good friends at that time, and we still are, she was in love with Percy Carson when we were teens."

"What happened to the girl in Chicago?" asked Emily.

"I thought about that girl for many years, and when I saw you at the slave auction, standing on that stage looking so delicate and pretty, I knew you were the woman I wanted to spend the rest of my life with," he said.

～

"I'm sorry about how it worked out. But after you got your inheritance, why didn't you go back to Chicago later and marry the girl?" Emily Asked.

"I could have done that, but I would have had to give up my inheritance and start another life somewhere else. I knew I couldn't do that. So I chose to keep my stay in bondage with my father's dreams, keep my inheritance, and marry my best friend Charlotte.

"Why did Madam Charlotte's father want to pay someone to marry her?" asked Emily. "Madam Charlotte is beautiful now, and must have been lovely as a girl."

"Charlotte had poor health, so her father thought no one wanted to marry her. She has a rare blood disease," he replied.

"So that's what causes her to feel tired and weak sometimes?" Emily stated.

"Yes, and that's why she needs you inside the house when the baby is born. She wants children, but it will be very dangerous for her to have a child. My plans were to wait until we had other doctors see Charlotte for another opinion because I was afraid that having a child could cause her to die, but she didn't want to wait any longer," he replied in a soft voice. "I think I got her pregnant the morning after you and I made love the first time. I was dreaming of you, and when I woke up, I had made love to her. I even called out your name, but I don't think she noticed."

"Hearing all these stories makes me love Madam Charlotte even more, and I don't want to hurt her in any way," said Emily.

"Then protect our secret forever and Charlotte will never know our love for each other," said Master Hoover. They started to walk back toward the main house. His wife was standing in the window waiting. "Emily, my darling, don't worry any more. Things will get better soon," Master Hoover said.

Emily felt better just talking to him. She had missed him so much and she really wanted to be with him alone soon, but it was very hard to arrange while she was living inside the big house.

Master Hoover knew that he needed to work out something because he had to keep Emily's mind on him. He never wanted to lose her affection. I could tell that he wanted to be with Emily as much as she wanted to be with him.

"Emily," Master Hoover said. His tone shifted to a serious one. "You must not walk alone any more. The baby is due any time, and I'm afraid you might get hurt. You know, I had to send Old Harry away to Mr. Montgomery's Plantation. I'm going to tell you the truth about him: I couldn't stand the thought of him being so close to you when you stayed in your quarters out back of the house late at night."

Enough truth, he had to tell her more lies.

"But Old Harry wasn't happy living here anyway because Sweet Anna had his child on the way, and he wanted to be a father."

Emily didn't say a word about that, she just kept on walking back toward the house. They passed by the barn as a mare was giving birth to her foal. Willie was taking care of her.

"Willie can help you when your baby is ready to come. Old doctor Pitts taught him all about the birth of horses, so he can deliver babies too."

Master Hoover went in the barn to see how the horse was doing. Emily stood by the door waiting. She wanted Master Hoover to ask her inside the barn and introduce her to Willie. She could tell that Master Hoover trusted him.

Willie was a tall, dark slave, a big man, handsome and extremely smart. Master Hoover asked Emily into the barn, and introduced her to Willie.

"Willie here's been on Hoover Ranch for over forty years, you know. He's partial to Miss Lilly."

It didn't matter to Willie that Miss Lilly was pregnant with Mr. Montgomery's child. He loved her. Willie had told Miss Lilly that he would be proud to marry her and be a father to her child.

"Now Emily, if you feel a need to walk at night, Willie will walk with you. But you're not allowed to walk alone any more."

Willie took her by the hand.

"Hello Miss Emily, pleased to meet you, I'll take you walking around the ranch any time you want," he said in his kind voice.

Willie had lived out back of the barn with Harry, but now that Harry was no longer around, he stayed there alone. Until Miss Lilly have the baby, though, he was staying with her.

Master Hoover was good to Willie because he could trust him. When the horses were sick or having a foal, no one could handle it better than Willie.

Willie had started working with the horses when he was only five years old. Master Hoover's father had sold Willie's parents when he was very young. He was only a baby, so other slaves helped raise him. Willie took to the horses at a young age and Dr. William Pitts noticed that he had a special touch with the animals and found himself growing fond of Willie. Dr. Pitts taught Willie all about taking care of sick horses and exactly what to do when a mare was having her foal.

By the time Master Hoover and Emily arrived back at the big house, Madam Charlotte was worried.

"Is anything wrong?" Emily asked.

"What took so long for you to return?"

"We stopped at the barn to watch a new foal being born; Emily wanted to see its birth. And I wanted to see if Willie needed any help," he said.

Then he told Madam Charlotte some lies about Harry. This led into his real plan. "Emily wants to go back to the nanny's quarters outside the big house so she can see more of Old Harry. It's late when he gets home in the middle of the night and Emily misses being with him," he said.

"Well, why does he get to the ranch so late?" Madam Charlotte wanted to know.

"He's got extra work over at Mr. Montgomery's place, and I owe Montgomery a favor so I have to let him work there. A deal's a deal," said Master Hoover.

"I'm sorry. I didn't mean to seem angry, but now that I understand what the problem is we'll work something out," said Madam.

"I can come in every morning when the babies are born," offered Emily.

"It sounds like a good idea for you and Harry to have your time together in the outside nanny's quarters," Madam Charlotte admitted. But she was afraid of being alone with a small baby. "You can't stay in the outside quarters when the babies are born," she said,

"Certainly, you and the babies will need a lot of care," Emily said. She knew that when the babies were born she'd need to move into the big house for at least two years. "But until then, if I can stay in the outside quarters, I can be with Harry," replied Emily.

Emily moved out back right away because she was hoping to see Master Hoover that night; but he knew that would look suspicious to his wife, so they waited until the following night. The next day, he couldn't wait to tell Madam Charlotte that the HMC Club was having a meeting that he needed to attend.

"I'll be gone most of the night. Willie will be in the front guardhouse to take care of you and Emily, if you need any help."

The only problem was that he was not going to any club meeting. He planned to see his lover. Emily was so happy to see him that she kissed and hugged him all night, but at about midnight as he was leaving, they heard a loud sound coming from the slave quarters. Master Hoover rushed to put on his pants and ran out back, leaving Emily behind. When he got there he found that it was Miss Lilly giving birth.

"Master, where is Willie?" asked Miss Lilly.

"Don't worry Lilly, I'll get him!"

Miss Lilly was doing fine, because she had help from some of the other slave women. She had been in labor all day and they'd been by her side. When Master Hoover saw what was going on, he ran to the guardhouse to get Willie. That's when he saw Percy Carson leaving the big house, but he was too excited to pay any attention. He kept on running to get Willie for Miss Lilly.

"Willie! Oh Willie! Miss Lilly is having the baby right now, and you must go to her." Willie went right away.

Master Hoover returned to Emily. "Miss Lilly is having her baby," he said, out of breath.

"I want to see if I can help," Emily said.

"My darling, in your condition you need to stay in your own quarters and remain calm. Miss Lilly has enough help, and you need to stay put, and you better relax because your own time is very close now."

Master Hoover started remembering about the night that his friend Mr. Montgomery had sex with Miss Lilly; he'd had sex with Emily for the first time that same night. Master Hoover thought that was

～

the night Miss Lilly got pregnant, and he wasn't sure if Emily got pregnant that same night. If so, he'd impregnated Emily and Madam Charlotte about the same time, so he thought, but Madam was having an affair with Percy too. He started to get worried about all the babies being born at once, so he stayed with Emily until she retired for the night and then kissed her and went back to the big house. He looked guilty, but Madam Charlotte had a guilty look on her face too.

She was all cleaned up, because she had just finished seeing her lover and this was her way of hiding the affair. She wore a big smile. Master Hoover suddenly remembered that he saw Percy Carson leaving the ranch, at least that's what he thought. It was late at night, and he couldn't see the gentleman caller's face in the dark. Master Hoover turned, looked at Madam Charlotte.

"Madam, was that Percy Carson I saw here at the ranch tonight?" he asked.

"Yes, it was Percy, he was looking for his brother Clifton, because he wanted to know about the HMC meeting."

Master Hoover suddenly remembered: the HMC meeting! Had Percy told her there really was no meeting?

"I told him you'd already left for the meeting, and the meeting was usually held at his house on the Carson Plantation." Master Hoover knew she was lying to him, but he was lying to her also. So he lied to Charlotte again and told her that the HMC meeting had been moved from the Carson Plantation to the Montgomery Plantation.

"When I got back from the meeting, I heard noise from the slave quarters and it was Miss Lilly having her baby, it must be close to your time?" he asked in a worried voice.

He remembered that she made love to him just a few hours after Master Montgomery had impregnated Miss Lilly, on that same night, and they had not made love to each other since. That made Master Hoover curious and he went on questioning Madam Charlotte.

"Is Percy Carson going to stay around here now that his mother has passed away and his brother is alone? Clifton can use some help running the place."

"I didn't ask Percy Carson anything," said Madam Charlotte, and she tried to change the subject.

"I thought Percy Carson was your lover once," Master Hoover commented. Madam Charlotte didn't say a word, she just walked out of the room.

On May 30, 1814, Miss Lilly had a fine baby girl, and she named her Rosa Carson because she planned to marry Willie Carson. Master Hoover went out back to see the baby, and he told them they should start planning their wedding; it was time to jump the broom.

When Master Hoover went to see Emily after Miss Lilly's baby was born, they talked about the baby's name and how cute she was. I was impressed with how happy Master Hoover was about the baby. I was still there, just watching.

One month later, on June 25, 1814, Willie came running in early in the morning, knocking on the door of the big house. Master opened the door.

"It's time," he said excitedly.

Master Hoover barely waking up. "What?" he replied.

"Emily's having her baby now. Miss Lilly is with her, she's in labor right now."

Just then Willie noticed a surprising thing—Master Hoover wasn't wearing any pants. When he ran into his room to get them, Madam Charlotte woke up from the noise.

"Emily's in labor. Miss Lilly's with her." He got dressed in a hurry and went to the outside nanny's quarters to see Emily, without Madam. The baby was born as soon as Emily saw Master Hoover's face in the doorway. He was a big boy, weighing over eight pounds.

"Beautiful. Just beautiful," Master Hoover said. "He looks like a white baby though, doesn't he to you?" he asked.

Emily just looked at him and smiled, not answering his question, and he smiled back at her.

Then Master Hoover picked up his firstborn son by his slave lover, just as proud as any father could be. He looked gratefully at Emily, feeling such love that it took his breath away. Emily wanted to put her

～

arms around him and kiss him. She was so proud of her son that she had tears in her eyes.

"What shall we name him?" she asked.

They decided to name their son Clarence Allen, using Emily's surname. He looked at the slave helpers and said, "You did a good job with Emily. I'm proud of my son and all of you," he told Willie and Lilly. "Watching you work with Emily is just like watching a real doctor. You're a good man." The proud father took the baby back to the big house in his arms. "Now, have Emily and her things moved into the main nanny's quarters right away. We need her in the house from now on."

Master Hoover took another look at his son's little face. When Willie brought Emily's things to her quarters, Master Hoover voiced a concern that had been bothering him. "I think Madam Charlotte is late on her delivery date. I want you to stay as close as possible to the main house. I was thinking she should have had her baby before Miss Lilly, and surely before Emily. Do you think it's because of her disease?"

Willie said nothing about Percy Carson's coming and going, he just shrugged his shoulders.

Master Hoover continued. "You need to go fetch Dr. Pitt as soon as possible when Madam Charlotte goes into labor." I was standing there watching and I heard what Master Hoover said to Willie. I wondered why Willie couldn't deliver Madam Charlotte's baby. Then I realized that it was because he was a colored man.

∽

When Master Hoover came back into the big house with the baby in his arms, Madam Charlotte could not wait to hold this baby in her arms. It was her first grandchild. At least, that's the way she felt. She opened the blanket, and saw that pretty face.

"This child is absolutely the prettiest baby I have ever seen, and it's a boy. Harry must be a happy man right now. I want to tell him that he did well by Emily. Did he give his son a name yet?" she asked.

Master Hoover was not happy about her saying that the baby was Harry's son, but he could not say that the baby was his.

"The child's name is Clarence Allen," he said.

Madam Charlotte was surprised and upset with Harry. "Why didn't he give the child his last name?" She said indignantly. "Clarence Allen Carson should be the boy's name," she said with concern.

"Well, Harry never liked the name Carson, so he wanted the child to carry Emily's last name. He said that the name Carson did not bring good memories to him.

Did you ever hear him use the name Carson before? No. He's always been called just plain Harry, ever since we've known him," said Master Hoover.

That wasn't enough explaining for Madam, so Master Hoover told her, "It was hurtful to Harry to think about the pain that his mother received from old man Carson, her master. Harry grew up with a lot of sad stories told to him about his Mama Sara. The truth is his mother received much pain for many years from both old Master Hoover and old man Carson."

Three weeks later in the middle of the night when Madam Charlotte was asleep, her water broke. She shook Master Hoover awake.

"The baby is coming!"

He ran down the hall right away to Emily's room, but was so excited he forgot to put on his pants. When he ran into the room he only had on his under shorts to tell her about Madam Charlotte; she was breast-feeding Clarence Allen.

What a beautiful sight, he thought. He stopped at the door and forgot what he came to tell her just that quick. He was standing there in the doorway looking at Emily with passion on his mind, thinking he needed to make love to her. When he came to himself, he tried to remember what it was that he came into Emily's room for. His mind was on kissing her, and making passionate love to her. Emily looked up and noticed him standing there without his pants on.

"What do you want?" she asked. Looking at him, she said, "Did you forget your pants?" They both laughed.

"You have the prettiest breasts that I've ever seen," he stuttered.

Emily realized that he had been standing there for a few minutes in his under shorts, watching her. The look in his eyes revealed his desires.

"Master Hoover, is there something that you

have to tell me, or do you want something from me?" Master Hoover stopped and thought about it. When he came to himself this time he remembered what he wanted.

"Oh my goodness, I am so sorry! Oh yes! Madam Charlotte is getting ready to have the baby."

Emily jumped up.

"Oh my, hurry, go get Willie to fetch the doctor, and tell Miss Lilly to come quickly!" Emily picked up Clarence Allen and went to her Madam's side right away. She carried Clarence Allen and laid him in one of the baby beds that Master Hoover had made for both babies. Clarence Allen was still asleep. She noticed that Madam Charlotte was in terrible pain, and when she saw Emily, she began to relax. She held out her hands to hold Emily's.

"I'm frightened. I think I may die because of my illness," she said

"Now don't you go worrying about anything, you're going to be all right. I'm going to take good care of you and the baby," Emily replied. She felt like this was the least that she could do for her Madam. "You took care of me when I was a young girl, now it's my turn to take care of you," Emily said.

"You still remember how it was when you were young?" Madam Charlotte asked, then said, "Emily I really do believe that you love me, and you are going to take good care of me, but I have something to talk to you about. It has been on my mind for some time now, and I feel that I must tell you now.

Emily, I have a secret to tell you that I have been carrying around for months now, that I have wanted to share with you."

I stood there speechless as she continued speaking her mind to Emily.

"I think it's time for me to talk to you about this, just in case I don't make it. Emily, Master Hoover and I are not in love with each other, and I don't think he is the father of this child that I am carrying." Emily was shocked, and Madam continued, "But Emily, I cannot tell him this at all. If I did, he would get rid of me. The truth is, I have been having an affair with Percy Carson ever since he returned home." Emily was speechless.

Then Madam Charlotte asked Emily to keep it a secret unless she died, and then she could do with the secret whatever she wished. I don't think Emily heard anything except that Master Hoover and Madam Charlotte were not in love with each other, and that they never had been.

Emily told her, "Madam your secret is safe with me forever." Then she put her arms around Madam. "Now relax, so the good Lord will give you peace, and then your baby can come into the world," Emily said with care.

Just as Madam Charlotte finished her conversation with Emily, Master Hoover walked into the room, and he seemed happy to see Emily comforting Madam Charlotte.

"I sent Willie to fetch Dr. Pitts," he said.

~

Miss Lilly came in with clean towels, hot water, and all the different oils that Dr. Pitts always used whenever he was delivering a baby. Emily and Miss Lilly cleaned up Madam Charlotte and she was all ready to give birth to her baby when the doctor arrived. Dr. Pitts came in and checked to see how far the baby had moved. The baby's head had dropped into the birth canal, and it was time to start pushing.

Something is wrong, Master Hoover was thinking. This baby is almost a month late. Dr. Pitts noticed him pacing the floor, and he knew that he was worried, so he told Master Hoover to go outside and wait until the baby was born.

Dr. Pitts knew he was not going to be able to take care of Madam Charlotte unless he got rid of Master Hoover. He had to think of a way to get him out of the way.

"Go wait with Willie, we'll call you when it's time to look at your new baby," said Dr. Pitts.

Willie was the doctor's favorite of all the slaves. When Willie's parents were sold off the Hoover plantation, he didn't even have a name. Dr. William Pitts really liked him, so he gave the child his first name: William. But they called him Willie.

Dr. Pitts was ready for the birth, but he was worried about Madam Charlotte, because he knew that she might have some real bad complications. Emily and Miss Lilly had already brought in all the things that Dr. Pitts needed for delivery. He always asked for a large bottle of whiskey, hot water, alcohol, peroxide, mineral oil, and some clean towels. He had everything there ready to go.

It looked like the baby was stuck. They could see the baby's head, but it just wouldn't come out. Emily stood up and grabbed Madam's legs. With Miss Lilly's help, they pulled Madam's legs all the way up over her head, and then they told her to push hard. Madam Charlotte pushed as hard as she could. And then it happened—the baby came.

Master Hoover was outside waiting with Willie. He was afraid his wife might die. He remembered what her father had said to him the day they got married. Madam Charlotte's father had been certain that if she had a baby, she would die in childbirth. Her father had told Master Hoover not to get Madam Charlotte pregnant. He started hearing her father's voice in his head.

"If you do get her with child, you had better pray, and pray hard. And if you want a son you should get one of your half-white slaves to bear him. Then take the boy and raise it as your own and keep your mouth closed."

Seeing the surprise on Master Hoover's face, Madam Charlotte's father had grown impatient. *"Boy! Learn to keep secrets, just like your old man did."* Old man Hoover had been known as "The Master of Deceit," a title that young Master Hoover had always wanted.

"No one will know the difference if your bed warmer

bears your son. We'll all think it's a white child by Charlotte. You can make it so."

~

Well, Master Hoover was trying to do just what his father-in-law suggested. He never wanted Madam Charlotte to become pregnant by him, but Madam had her own plan.

I didn't want her to go though this pain, or take any chance of dying, he said in his mind. Then he heard the baby crying and that made him happy because he thought everything was all right with Madam Charlotte.

When he went into the room the doctor told him the bad news. "Your baby is fine, but Madam Charlotte isn't out of the woods yet, it's been a long, hard procedure, and we almost lost her," the doctor said.

Master Hoover stood in the doorway looking at the three of them and noticed Emily holding a blue blanket in her arms with what looked like a new baby.

"Come look at your son, and then we can talk about your wife's care and answer any questions that you may have," said Dr. Pitts.

Master Hoover walked over to look at his new son, and took him from the arms of his lover. As he looked into the face of his second son, he thought about the morning that he thought this son was conceived.

Master Hoover thought that this baby was born late, perhaps causing Madam Charlotte to have such a hard time giving birth. As he stood, deep in

~

thought, Dr. Pitts called him, trying to get his attention. Master Hoover finally heard his name,

"I'm sorry? I was thinking about a name for my son."

"Madam will need at least three to five weeks of careful care to survive this ordeal, and she's lost a lot of blood and is still bleeding. I had to use a lot of packing in the birth wound, but I haven't entirely stopped the bleeding," the doctor said. He turned to Emily and Miss Lilly, "You must change the packing every day to keep from setting up any kind of infection."

"Is my wife going to die?" Master Hoover asked, giving the baby to Emily.

"That is not up to me. I assure you I will do everything in my power to save her, but she faces a long, hard battle," said Dr. Pitts. They all knew it was going to take lots of prayer and hope for Madam Charlotte to survive.

"I'm willing to cooperate in any way that is needed to help Charlotte get well, she is my best friend, and Dr. Pitts, I would do anything to keep her on this ranch with us. I need to keep her from dying," said Master Hoover.

I was surprised to hear him refer to Madam Charlotte as his best friend. I was still there watching, but this was one of my saddest days. I thought Master Hoover could be a good person sometimes, but I couldn't believe that at a time like this he could call her his best friend.

"We'll do the best we can." That's all Dr. Pitts

~

would say. The doctor had given Madam Charlotte a large dose of whiskey for her pain, so Master Hoover had no chance to talk with her, and he was not happy about that.

Well, everyone had a job to do to save Madam Charlotte's life. In order to get her well, they had to work together. Emily's job was to take care of the babies, and that was fine with her, but she wanted to be near Madam Charlotte also. Emily brought both of the babies into Madam's room so they could all be near each other. Emily breast-fed the babies and she watched Madam Charlotte sleep. She also thought that if Madam could hear the babies crying, it might strengthen her will to fight for life.

Master Hoover knew how much Emily loved Madam Charlotte. I guess he was trying to be a loving friend, husband or whatever he thought he was to the Madam, but I wondered if he did it just so he could keep himself looking good in Emily's eyes.

Miss Lilly's job was to make sure Madam Charlotte had a good meal every day, and that was easy for her, since she was the house cook. Miss Lilly had a small baby of her own, and between cooking and breast-feeding her own baby, she was exhausted. Every day Miss Lilly made Madam Charlotte chicken broth soup, and every day she put the soup in a bottle and laid Madam's head in her lap to feed the soup to her. Madam Charlotte was unable to feed herself, so Miss Lilly fed her like a baby.

Dr. Pitts was a great friend and a fine doctor. He

changed her packing every day, and when he wasn't there Emily or Miss Lilly did it, which kept her from getting infections. The doctor even slept outside her room, day and night.

Three weeks passed with no change in Madam's condition. Master Hoover and Willie were very worried.

"I need to get her well so she can see her beautiful baby," Master Hoover told Willie.

Willie knew that Master Hoover was very worried about Madam so he stayed with him all the time, always very supportive to Master. They all wanted her to see her beautiful son, the child that she had always wanted.

One day, Master Hoover went into Madam's room, and he just stood there looking at her. He called out for Emily to come into the room with him. Master Hoover wanted to give his son a name but he didn't know if Madam Charlotte had selected a name for him already.

I had noticed Emily outside the closed door talking to Willie. She was asking him to help her think of something to get Madam Charlotte well again.

Master Hoover was asked to sign his son's birth record for filing in the town hall of records. So, he had to give his son a name. Emily heard him calling her name. She came into Madam's room hoping that she was better, but she wasn't.

"Do you know if Charlotte has chosen a name?" asked Master Hoover.

He tried to pretend that he wanted to see her about naming his son, but she noticed Master Hoover looking at her with passion in his eyes. When Emily looked into his eyes she knew that he really wanted her body badly.

No sooner than Emily had entered the room, he reached out his arms to hold her.

"Master Hoover, please, let's not do this now. Our Madam is ill and this is neither the time nor the place to think about ourselves. I can't think of anything but Madam Charlotte at this time."

He still wanted more, but Master Hoover knew that he had no choice but to stop, unless he wanted to lose Emily for good. This would be unbearable, especially since there was already a great possibility that he may be losing Madam Charlotte. He changed to a safer subject.

"But did she say anything about naming the baby?"

"Madam Charlotte told me that she liked the name Joel Edward, and she had planned to discuss that name with you soon, but I guess she never got the chance."

"Then it's done. My son will be Joel Edward Hoover."

This son was born on July 25, 1814, just one month after Emily's son Clarence Allen was born. It was so touching to see how much Emily loved the woman that she felt was the only mother that she knew. I believed she would have stopped loving Master Hoover if he did anything to hurt Madam Charlotte.

∼

Four weeks later, and with no improvement in Madam's health, Emily called a meeting. She assembled
Dr. Pitts, Willie, Miss Lilly, and Master Hoover.

"It is now four weeks and Madam Charlotte's
condition has not improved, she is still very weak.
We have got to do something, or we may lose her
soon. There is only one more thing that I can think
of, and that is an 'Unbreakable Chain Prayer, the
believers' prayer.'" Colored families did this prayer
all over the South when they had serious illness in
their homes.

"Emily, tell me how this believer's prayer works?"
asked Master Hoover.

"The whole family will join hands in a circle
and then an appointed family member will lead the
prayer to God. That person is called 'The Believer.'
The Believer must be a true believer in God."

Master Hoover took a look around in Madam's
room and walked to her bedside. As he watched
her, the pain showed in his eyes. Emily was glad
to see him thinking about doing the prayer, even if
he decided against it. As long as Emily had known
him, he had never prayed, or even gone to church.
Then Master Hoover looked at everybody in the
room, even the babies who were still asleep. He
reached down to touch his son, who was sleeping
by Madam, gently on his head.

"What would I need to do?" he asked.

"Master Hoover, you would have to truly believe in the power of God," said Emily quietly.

"Emily! Let's do it!" He looked around the room again. "I want Emily to be The Believer," he said.

Master Hoover didn't know that all the other slaves out back on the plantation were joining hands, in preparation for Emily's prayer. One by one, the people in the room and the slaves on Hoover Ranch joined hands.

"You all must listen to me very carefully! No matter what happens, don't let go of anyone's hand, until the prayer is completed," Emily paused, because the next instruction was very important. "The circle must not be broken by anyone." Then Emily closed her eyes and began to pray.

My Dear Divine Father, here we all are, coming into your heavenly home, knocking on your door, with a joint prayer from all of us. We are asking you to help us please. I don't think we even deserve a favor from you, but we are asking you anyway.

We know that you are a forgiving God. We are all asking for your forgiveness in our wrongdoings, my Lord. We are not coming to you totally for ourselves today, but we are asking for Madam Charlotte. She has not sinned as we have, so please, Lord, don't let her die. If it is your will, dear Lord, to take Madam Charlotte home with you at this time, then we accept it fully and completely without question. But Lord, what we have done under your sight, we know it was wrong, so please, dear God, forgive us and make us better. We are a family and we love each other. We come to you asking you to find consolation in your power to give Madam Charlotte back to her newborn son, and us.

We are asking you, Lord, if it's your will. We love you Lord. Amen!

At the end of the Believer's Prayer, everyone held hands for a moment. And then they heard a voice.

"Where is my baby?" They all turned around, it was Madam Charlotte, sitting up in her bed, and by a miracle she was talking and smiling again! She reached her arms out for her child.

"Thank you all for taking good care of me and my baby, and especially you, Emily, my daughter," she said to Emily.

As soon as she could, Emily went out back to thank the slaves for their prayers, telling them that Madam Charlotte would be all right now. That made them happy and they started celebrating by singing with Sister Harriet leading a very beautiful old gospel hymn, right outside of Madam Charlotte's window.

In spite of the slave's loud songs of celebration, the babies drifted off to sleep. The singing lifted everyone's spirits and put the babies to sleep at the same time. When they noticed that the babies relaxed to the singing, Emily and Madam Charlotte asked Sister Harriet to sing outside the window every night.

Dr. Pitts was amazed at the way Madam Charlotte came out of her illness. When he finished his examination he said, "It is a miracle."

He told everyone that she was out of the woods and back to her old self again. Master Hoover decided to throw a big celebration party, inviting all of their friends, and he also planned to give a party out back for all of the slaves, as soon as Madam Charlotte was on her feet and feeling stronger.

CHAPTER 5

For the next two weeks, they kept Madam Charlotte in bed because the doctor said that she needed to build up her strength. When Master Hoover heard that Madam Charlotte was going to be bedridden, it was very disappointing to him.

Master Hoover had started to plan her party, and he was already planning to spend some of his evenings with Emily having sex late into the night. Emily wasn't thinking of sex. She had planned to spend lots of time in Madam's room, catching up on news and playing with their babies.

"Tell me everything I missed during the last few weeks," Madam Charlotte urged.

Emily smiled at her and said, "Master Hoover was dreadfully worried, and so was the doctor, also Willie, Miss Lilly, Master Hoover, and all the slaves on the plantation joined in the Believer's Prayer,"

"I had a dream during my illness. I was looking at all of you from a high place, it seemed. It was like looking at everyone in a mirror. I heard you calling me back, but I didn't want to come, until I saw the face of my son." Madam said.

Madam Charlotte told how she was not able to

speak during her illness, but she could hear everything around her.

Emily thought perhaps the doctor had overmedicated Madam, thinking the pain would be too much for her to handle. Then Madam Charlotte thought about the secret that she had told before the birth of her son, the one about Percy Carson.

"Did you tell anyone about the secret?" she asked. This upset Emily, because she had forgotten about the secret.

"What was it about, Madam? I've forgotten it and I am sorry for forgetting. I had so much on my mind that it was impossible to remember all of the things I was told, with you so sick."

"Was it so bad?" asked Madam Charlotte.

"Yes, you were very ill for many weeks, and I was so busy with feeding the babies, and trying to eat the right foods to have enough milk for both of them, and also worrying about losing you."

Madam Charlotte wanted to make sure Emily had really forgotten what she had confided about Percy. She looked at her closely.

"Madam, it was hard to remember anything, and I would never want to forget anything you told me." Emily said sadly.

Relieved, Madam Charlotte said, "Oh don't you worry about that because it wasn't important anyway."

Emily felt just awful that Madam Charlotte had told her something to remember, and she had forgotten what it was.

"It must be a sign of aging," Emily said. Madam looked at her and said,

"Although you are only twenty-one years old," then they both laughed.

Two days later, Emily was just finishing up feeding both boys and putting them down for the night. Both boys slept in Madam's room because Emily wanted to stay near her. They were spending a lot of time together and Master Hoover was starting to feel replaced. This was not making him happy, so one night he decided to go out on the town.

"I'm going to my friend's plantation for the HMC meeting," he told the two women.

They were having one of those betting games with the slaves and that usually lasted all night. He wanted to go because he was not getting any attention from Emily or Madam Charlotte. As he left for the meeting, he thought he was going to have some big fun that night, but when he got there all he could think about was Emily. Watching the sex game with the slaves, two couples from the fields, didn't do him any good. When the sex game started he wanted Emily even more, and he was thinking about getting up and going home, but he thought Emily would be busy with Madam.

Emily and Madam Charlotte had been talking and playing with the boys all day and night. Well, Emily was finally very tired and so was Madam Charlotte because she fell asleep while Emily was talking to her. Emily got up and checked on both of the babies and found them both asleep. It was good that they were asleep because Emily was very sleepy herself.

Emily noticed that she was the only one awake so she decided to go to her quarters to freshen up. She wanted to get some sleep herself. She took a bath in her washroom and put on one of her sexy nightgowns. Emily felt sexual after finishing her bath but she knew that Master Hoover was out for the evening. Emily's son was three months old, and she had not made love in five months. Just as she got in the bed, Master Hoover entered her room. When he noticed that she saw him, he walked closer to her bed.

Emily opened her arms to him, and he went into them so gently that their bodies might have been two magnets, the way that they linked together. He wrapped his lips around her soft tender lips and they kissed each other with intense desire, turning on the fire until her body was like a hot sauna. His body began to sweat, as she looked into his eyes with such sensuality that it made him want her even more. They melted into each other with a burning need, which caused an intense, emotionally compelling and electrifying climax, ending with a gentle feeling of acceptance.

This was a night of great love for them. Master Hoover held Emily in his arms and kissed her all night. This was the first time they had actually spent the whole night together. The next morning they looked out into the daylight together in bed.

"I love you," he said drowsily.

Emily was pleased as she looked into his eyes. "You are my world," she said. They kissed each other.

"I have to leave to check on the boys," Emily said later, getting up to dress. She went into the changing room where the water pan and bath towels were and began to wash herself all over. Master Hoover was watching Emily clean her body and soon found himself wanting more of her. He was getting aroused just watching her wash herself, and by the time she came out ready to go work, he wanted her again badly.

She wore a pretty, white cotton dress that he could see the shape of her body through. Master Hoover couldn't stop himself. Before he knew it he had reached out and grabbed Emily, pulling her close, kissing her. His desire started to rise until he couldn't wait; he wanted her right then.

Suddenly, she heard Miss Lilly outside her door calling for her, so they had to stop. Emily started laughing when she looked at his face because it showed so much disappointment. She went to the door and Miss Lilly was standing there, "Madam Charlotte is awake and asking for you," she called through the closed door.

"I'll be there soon, I'm almost dressed," answered Emily.

Miss Lilly went back and told Madam Charlotte that Emily had overslept and was on her way.

"Miss Lilly, I thought Emily was spending the night in my room last night."

Madam Charlotte thought since Master Hoover

was gone all night with his gambling friends, Emily would stay with her and the children.

"When I woke up and missed Emily I started looking for her, even though the babies were still asleep. Do you know where she went?" She asked.

"No, Madam," answered Miss Lilly.

Emily got ready to leave Master Hoover, looking back at him and smiling. "It's some cold water in the bath that might cool you off, and I will see you later." Then she walked out the door.

He laughed at her, sat on her bed, picked up her pillow, and held it close to his body. He could smell her on the pillow and he began to hold the pillow as if he was holding her in his arms tenderly. She softly touched him in her mind through the door.

"Good day, my love," she whispered, and walked away.

Emily went into Madam's room and the boys were still asleep. Madam Charlotte was wide-awake and very happy indeed to see Emily.

"I missed you. Did you forget Master Hoover was going to be out all night?"

Just as Emily was getting ready to answer, Master Hoover walked in. He went to the boys and gave a great fatherly pat to each of their heads. He left to take a bath and changed for a business meeting with the Plantation Association Group. This was an organization started by the plantation owners to discuss the laws of slavery. They talked about the price of slaves, the trading of slaves, and the war that was getting ready to put an end to slavery.

Suddenly time started to pass fast. I found myself spinning around, like flying through thin air, and when I stopped things were different. Master Hoover was outside talking to his son, who looked to be no more than nine years old.

"You can only play with Emily's boy, not the other slave children," Master Hoover told his son. Joel Edward thought Emily was his father's sister, one of the first lies that Master Hoover told him. But what did it matter? Joel was just a young boy; he loved Emily. He thought her son was his cousin.

Clarence Allen was Emily's first son. Her second son, Willie Leroy Allen, was born March 20, 1815, and now was four years old. He was named after her Miss Lilly's husband Willie. By now, Miss Lilly had become Emily's best friend. David Roy Allen, Emily's third son was born on January 15, 1816. At this time, he was three years old. *Master Hoover can't keep his hands off her*, I thought. He was getting her pregnant every year, and in 1816 it was twice in the same year. Emily's fourth son, Peter Joe Allen, was also born in 1816, on December 28. He was two years old, soon to be three. One cute little boy played alone. He looked like he was only one year old. This was Emily's fifth son, Evan Lee Allen, born October 19, 1817.

I looked over by the big house and saw a baby

in Madam Charlotte's arms. He was Emily's sixth son, Joey Jon Allen, born on July 25, 1818. Because he was born on the birthday of Madam Charlotte's only son, Madam named this child. As I watched, Madam Charlotte turned to take the baby inside.

Since Clarence Allen was the oldest, Master Hoover told him that he was responsible for the others, even Madam Charlotte's son Joel Edward. He was responsible for something else, too; whenever Master Hoover wanted to have sex with Emily, he sent Clarence Allen out back near the barn to watch all of his brothers, so he wouldn't be interrupted.

Master Hoover was in his late fifties by this time, and Emily was still in her early twenties. Emily still excited him because of her beauty and youth. I remember thinking men are very strange sometimes because Charlotte was in her late forties, and she too was a very beautiful lady. Maybe it was true that they'd never been in love. One thing was certain: when it came to Emily, he was head over heels.

I was sad when Dr. Pitts told Master Hoover and Madam Charlotte the sad news. But it was probably for the best.

"If you ever get pregnant again you would surely die in childbirth," said Dr. Pitts firmly. They weren't surprised, but she still wanted more children.

He'd had enough of the whole business with her, and didn't want to father any more children with her. On the other hand, he was concerned about having only one son to carry the Hoover name into the future. What if this son had only daughters? The Hoover name would be no more.

Emily was giving him one son after the next, but they were Allens, so he started working on a plan. Master Hoover thought about what old man Montgomery said about fathering his children with a mulatto slave girl and raising them as his own white children. This was beginning to sound like a good idea.

Even though she had hoped for more children, Madam Charlotte felt blessed with her one son; she knew that she could have met death during the birth of any child. Of course, she also thought of the family name going into the future. She loved playing grandmother to Emily's sons.

Madam Charlotte often thought what kind of a father Harry was turning out to be. She wondered why he wasn't spending more time with the boys. She didn't know he was living with Sweet Anna by now, and that she was pregnant with his fourth child. Master Hoover told all the slaves that Harry was living with another woman on the Montgomery Plantation, but ordered them not to speak of it to Madam Charlotte. The Master of Deceit always gave a reason that sounded good. He told the slaves not to tell her anything because she was so fond of Harry.

Madam Charlotte thought that Harry was still working for the Montgomery Plantation during the day, and that he came home at night, and that every year he was getting Emily pregnant. She thought for a long time that something was wrong with the story, but she was so busy with her own love affair that she didn't pay close attention.

One day Madam Charlotte noticed that Emily and her husband had a secret. She start to notice that when around Master Hoover, Emily was acting like a woman in love. She certainly wasn't acting like he was her father. Around Master Hoover, Emily always smelled like a flower. Around Master Hoover, she wore her nice dresses. But what really made Madam Charlotte wonder was that Emily never seemed to be around Harry, and didn't even speak to him when he was there. Madam Charlotte knew something was wrong with that picture, and thought for a long time that it just didn't feel right the stories they were telling her. She'd been secretly seeing Percy for almost six years, and Master Hoover seemed happy all the time.

Aha! she thought to herself. *Harry isn't the father of Emily's children because he isn't around the ranch enough to get her pregnant.* She knew this wasn't like the Harry that she remembered. Then she remembered that Emily had moved inside the big house when her sixth child was born, and Master Hoover would never let Harry inside the big house to be with Emily in bed.

Oh, who am I trying to fool? Madam admitted to herself. *I have known about my husband's love for her ever since the day he brought her here, I just didn't want to believe it. Besides, I needed her myself since I didn't have Percy and didn't love Master Hoover as a husband. Raising her as a daughter filled my empty life.*

Because her affair with Percy kept Madam happy, she really didn't care. But then she thought, *One day they'll know I was never fooled by their affair. Master Hoover, I am the master of deceit. I know about you, but you don't know about me.* She knew everything, but she accepted it.

Madam Charlotte recalled the day of the Unbreakable Chain Prayer. They thought she couldn't hear, but she was just drunk from all the whiskey the doctor had given her for pain. Now, six years later, it all came back to her.

Emily was the believer who led the prayer for me when I was sick. They all thought I was asleep, well I wasn't, and I could hear everything, even Emily's confession that she made to God for having an affair with Master.

It took Madam Charlotte six years to decipher what was going on around her during the time she was sick. Recollections came back to her about Emily and Master Hoover talking in her room one day.

"Madam Charlotte means more to me than having sex with you," Emily had said. Yes, Emily was her daughter, who loved her.

Madam Charlotte knew of her husband's affair with Emily, but she didn't know that Emily remembered her confession about Percy. Even though Emily felt making love to Master Hoover was wrong, she could not stop. The confession gave Emily some comfort.

≈

Madam Charlotte found out about many of the lies that had been told to her over the years. She knew her health was fragile; if she said anything, it could cause lot of trouble with her husband, plus she didn't want to be without Emily and the boys.

Madam Charlotte knew she could stay with Percy Carson, her lover, or with her brother Frederick, but neither was young enough to take care of her when she got old and weak. Two things Madam Charlotte realized she could count on: Emily's love and the love of her only son Joel Edward. But only Emily would be there all her life to care for her.

Since this was a day of remembering, Madam Charlotte started to think about her father. She'd heard him, years ago, talking to old man Hoover in the barn. She heard her father tell old man Hoover that he'd saved up over $10,000 to give to him.

> "I've saved all this money over the last five years to buy my little Charlotte a life. Now if you would arrange the marriage between your only son and my only little girl, this money is all yours," he said. "It's not like they don't know each other," said old Man Hoover. "They've been good friends all their lives." He thought a bit. "Well my good friend, what about your girl's health? And Montgomery, what about the boy your girl is dating, old William Carson's son?" "True, she is a sickly little thing, but my Charlotte is a fine looking woman. He may be able to get one child out of her, but then again the doctor did say she shouldn't get pregnant because of

her blood disease." Mr. Montgomery had to think a bit to come up with an answer for the first question, but the second answer came instinctively. "And Hoover, you know I'd as soon as die before I let my only daughter marry in that old rat's family."

Listening to them describe her frailties, and the boy she loved, had been painful for Charlotte. Percy Carson's father wasn't going to arrange for her to marry his son either, because he didn't like Mr. Montgomery any more than Montgomery liked him. She knew she'd never change their minds. Edward Dennis Hoover was her best friend, anyway.

How bad can it be? she asked herself. *I'll be married to a good-looking man like Edward Hoover, and I'll be rich, too.* All the girls in town wanted him, so better her than them, she thought, since she wouldn't be able to marry her true love. *I can make him fall in love with me after our marriage,* she thought, and she hoped she'd learn to love him too.

Master Hoover didn't know what his father had done until the marriage was arranged. Charlotte wasn't going to be the one to tell him. She kept the conversation she heard in the barn a secret. Although, she didn't know Master Hoover had thought about all this, and had his own secrets.

His father told him that he couldn't marry the half-white colored girl from Chicago, and if he disobeyed he would be disinherited. If he couldn't have the woman he loved, he'd didn't care about women or a wife. He'd do whatever his father told

~

him to do in order to keep his inheritance. He had secret thoughts too.

He decided. *Somewhere down the line I'll have a bed warmer and I'll choose a light-skinned colored girl, even if I have to cheat on my wife.* He was determined to be happy, but he hadn't planned on falling in love with a bed warmer. If he had to be in an arranged marriage, he was glad it was with his best friend. Although he tried to learn to be her lover, it wasn't enough.

So her marriage had been full of lies from Master Hoover, but she couldn't get angry. Actually she was happy. She'd known all along that Master Hoover would have someone else.

Why not Emily? she'd thought. *He now loved a woman that cared even more about her, and it kept him home most of the time. In his mind, Emily is the girl in Chicago. He'll never leave me, and neither will Emily.* In a way, she was winning. She thought she was playing the same game as Master Hoover.

One day, far in the future, Madam Charlotte planned to tell Emily that she had always known about Master Hoover fathering her sons. Before Emily, Madam Charlotte didn't feel that her life mattered to anyone. When Emily became her daughter, everything changed. Emily had six wonderful sons who were now part of Madam Charlotte's life; whenever she felt lonely, she would call all the boys into the house and play games with them. She taught them how to read. Right along with Master Hoover, Madam Charlotte was planning the future for their grandsons.

Master Hoover and Madam Charlotte were making plans to ensure the children's survival after slavery was over. They filed documents in the hall of records stating the boys were white, the ultimate secret. After that, it was up to them to continue living on the ranch and keep their secrets.

Other states had already freed their slaves. Even though all of Emily's sons were kept a secret from the world, and could pass for white, the Hoovers felt there was still some risk for them.

Master Hoover loved his boys, and he treated them like they were white. He thought Madam Charlotte was proud of the way he treated the boys and was hoping that Madam Charlotte thought he was acting like a proud grandfather, because he still thought he had her fooled.

They never allowed the boys off the plantation for any reason, bringing everything they needed to the plantation for them. They only played with children on Hoover Ranch. When the Hoovers had parties and when visitors came to the plantation, the boys were taken out of sight.

The guards were instructed to keep them from being seen, so they hid the boys. When they grew up, the boys had a choice to pass for white, or to acknowledge their colored heritage. Only Dr. Pitts, the slaves, and close friends who were slave owners themselves knew the boys even existed. People in town thought the Hoovers were private people because the ranch was built in a way to keep their private life secret.

There were rumors about a newspaperman in town years ago. Someone said that the newspaperman captured a slave named Willie from Hoover's Ranch, who'd been in town running an errand for Old Man Hoover, Sr.

When Old Man Hoover, Sr., found out that the owner of the newspaper had tortured Willie for information on the Hoovers, just so he could write an article about the Hoovers' private life in his newspaper, he was furious. The slave made it back to the ranch beaten close to death, rumor had it, but he was able to tell Master Hoover who had hurt him: a man Hoover knew was the owner of the Morning Sun Newspaper.

"What did he want to know from you?" Old Man Hoover asked.

"All about what went on inside the walls of Hoover Ranch. That's what he asked about," said Willie.

Old Man Hoover went to see the owner of the newspaper.

"If you write one word, you say anything about my family in your paper or you ever put your hands on any slave of mine again, then you won't live to read your own paper the next day." He told him.

Well, the newspaperman did indeed write a story the next day. He led right off with: *Master Edward D.*

~

Hoover Sr., owner of the Hoover Ranch Plantation, is a deceitful man. He has built a prison of secrets behind that brick wall he calls a home. The article went on to say:

> Secrets are being kept by everybody, even the slaves, and there may well be some illegal business going on behind those tall gates. Old Man Hoover threatened to kill this newspaperman if he wrote anything in his paper about his family or his slaves.
>
> In this reporter's opinion, he is a nigger lover.

The next day the newspaperman didn't show up for work, and a copy of the paper sat on his desk unread. Just like old man Hoover said, he never got a chance to read his own article. He never showed up for work again, and he was never found.

The Hoover's never had any trouble after that. No one tried to get through the walls of the Hoover Ranch Plantation or tell any of their secrets. No one knew anything about the Hoover family tree except the Hoovers themselves, but after the newspaperman disappeared, people seemed to feel a lot less curious. The slaves knew better than to speak of any family business. They'd been told that if they opened their mouths, they would be killed on the spot by the guards, on orders from Old Man Hoover.

I felt sleepy again. Just as I drifted off, I was awakened by another noise.

It was 1820. I heard a lot of noise in the nanny's house out back where Emily lived. It was Emily and

Master Hoover making love to each other. The children were just outside the door playing. I saw Emily's firstborn son, Clarence Allen, taking the boys away. He was remembering his orders given by Master Hoover.

He knew to take his brothers a way from the groaning sounds, and he'd moved them out by the barn as far as possible, so they couldn't hear anything. He even told him to take Joel Edward, if he was around. Clarence Allen was told that they were playing a grown-up game together. He knew that the game took a long time, sometimes most of the day. So when the noises began he headed for the barn to spend time with Willie, who was tending to the horses.

I saw Willie and Miss Lilly and I was happy to see them. It looked like they were married; at least they were living together. Then I saw a very beautiful, white girl standing in Miss Lilly's door. She was looking out at Clarence Allen. I could tell that she liked him by the way that she watched him. When the boys went over to the barn where the horses were she came running out of the house, running over to Willie who was putting a shoe on one of the horses.

"Father, what are you doing?" she said. I was surprised because she couldn't be Willie's daughter.

Willie looked down at her and said, "Rosa, how many times you seen me do this?" She laughed.

"I know, Father, but tell me anyway!"

Willie saw Clarence Allen with all of his brothers walking toward them.

∼

"Oh! Rosa, not this again, why don't you just tell Clarence that you like him?"

Rosa looked at her father, and said, "Father, that wouldn't be ladylike!"

"Okay, I will do it for you," said Willie. Rosa started laughing because she didn't believe him.

Looking out the barn door at the boys, Willie realized that Master Hoover was having his way with Emily. He went out and talked to Clarence Allen.

"Do you boys want to come in the barn and watch me put a shoe on the horse?"

They were excited about watching, especially Evan Lee. He really loved the horses from the first time he saw them, even though he was barely three years old. Master Hoover spent a lot of time showing off his sons to the slaves and teaching them about the horses. The boys went inside with Willie.

Clarence Allen was six years old, but he was a very mature six-year-old. Madam Charlotte used to say that he was beyond his years. This was the day he got to know Rosa. She was already interested in him, and as time went by they got to be very good friends, to the point that when they grew up they got married.

Master Hoover and Emily were still having sex in the nanny's quarters when Madam Charlotte came out of the big house onto the porch. She was looking for the boys, afraid they had wandered off, but they were in the barn with Willie. Rosa saw Madam Charlotte standing out on the porch.

≈

"Clarence, I think your grandmother is looking for you," she said. He walked out of the barn and looked across the way.

"Grandmother, are you looking for us?" he asked in a loud voice.

"You boys come on up to the porch," she called back.

Clarence Allen went into the barn to get his brothers to take them home. Madam Charlotte wanted to tell them that Joel was home from school and ready to play with Clarence Allen, as they did every day after school. Joel went to school in town because he was white. The guards took him to town to school and they brought him back every day after school. The others boys were home schooled, because they were kept secret from the community.

I thought Madam Charlotte could hear Master Hoover and Emily having sex in the nanny's quarters, especially when she looked out toward the nanny's quarters as she was calling the boys, but she didn't say anything. After she got the boys in the house, she played with the smaller boys while Joel and Clarence Allen played together.

CHAPTER 6

I found myself falling off to sleep again. It seemed like I was getting sleepy all the time. This time when I woke up I heard something that sounded like crying. I opened my eyes as quickly as I could.

Oh my goodness it's Emily, it looks like she's pregnant again. I could tell it was late at night. I saw Master Hoover trying to have sex with this very pregnant woman, and then I thought, *My oral history stated she only had seven children. This must be her last child because she has had six sons already.*

I couldn't believe that Master Hoover was having sex with her, because she looked like she was in her ninth month. I looked again. Oh my goodness, it looked like her water broke! First, he thought she was still enraptured as he was, but then he noticed she was crying. Soon he figured out that she was crying because of the pain that she was having from the contractions. The baby was coming. He didn't know what to do, so he held her in his arms trying to comfort her.

I wanted to help, so I ran over to Miss Lilly's quarters and tried to wake her up, but I couldn't make any noise. I was just walking through walls, like a fool. I tried to wake Willie, but with no luck there either, and I found myself getting anxious. I ran over to the big house to try to wake Madam Charlotte, and I was surprised that she heard me fall through the door. I felt the door move through my body, and saw Madam Charlotte jump up like she heard me. That's when she noticed Master Hoover wasn't in bed next to her.

She went to the window and looked out and heard crying. After finding her robe and slippers, she threw them on while running out the door to Willie's quarters, and this time he heard the knock on his door.

"Willie, you must come now, I think Emily is having the baby and there may be problems, so come quickly!" This was the first time Madam Charlotte had ever been out back in the slave quarters.

I wondered why she didn't go to the nanny's quarters first and then I realized that she knew Master Hoover was in there trying to have sex with Emily.

Madam Charlotte didn't want him to know that she had always known what was going on, and she wanted to give him enough time to put on his pants. After she fetched Willie, she went to Emily's door and knocked. Master Hoover had gotten his clothes on by that time. The boys were awake.

I could tell she wanted to get rid of Master Hoover, to be alone with Emily.

"Master, please take the children to Pastor Martin's quarters and see what's taking Willie and Miss

Lilly so long to get here." As soon as he left, she went over to Emily to comfort her. Emily was giving birth to her seventh son on Madam Charlotte's birthday, which made her very happy.

Master Hoover dropped the boys at Pastor Martin's quarters and went to fetch Willie and Miss Lilly again. When they arrived, the baby was almost born; all Willie had to do was guide the baby out. Madam Charlotte had walked Emily right through the birth of her seventh son. Master Hoover looked guilty.

"Uh, Madam Charlotte, I heard a noise earlier and it sounded like crying, so I came over to see if my help was needed." Master Hoover was trying to come up with an explanation as to why he was in Emily's room. "When I left, you were sleeping and I didn't want to wake you." Madam Charlotte let him go on and on with his explaining, but she knew the truth.

I was surprised they let Madam Charlotte stay in the slave quarters while Emily was having the baby. Maybe Master Hoover was just too ashamed to tell her to leave. After all, it was her birthday and he didn't want to hurt her feelings. The baby was another son, and Madam Charlotte was proud. This child looked much like Joel Edward, Madam's son.

"This one is mine," said Madam Charlotte. Emily looked up in surprise. "His name is Edward Leon Hoover."

This was the only one of Emily's sons that was given the Hoover name, and the only one that was raised in the big house as a white child.

Master Hoover privately wished that he had given all of his sons the name Hoover, especially after finding out that Madam Charlotte couldn't have any more children. Madam Charlotte wrapped him up.

"Get Emily cleaned up and bring her and her things into the big house to the master bedroom," she said to Miss Lilly, as she walked out with the baby.

She turned and took the baby to the big house, and went straight to the bedroom where she placed little Edward Leon in her son's old bed, the same one she used when Joel was a baby. He was to sleep right next to her.

Emily was too tired to feel hurt or sad. Little Edward Leon Hoover was going to stay in the big house. Master Hoover told all of the slaves on the plantation that Madam Charlotte had given birth to another child to cover his next lie, which was to raise this child as his own, as a white child.

When they got over to the big house with Emily, Master Hoover and Madam Charlotte were both waiting with the baby. By the time Emily got there, she accepted the idea that they wanted to raise him as a Hoover. Emily thought that giving her seventh son to the woman who had raised her like a mother was the least she could do. Madam Charlotte didn't have Master Hoover's love, she couldn't have babies anymore, and she couldn't be with her true love, Percy Carson. Emily felt like she gave some happiness to Madam Charlotte when she gave her another baby to care for as her own.

Besides, Emily was deeply in love with Master Hoover and they were starting to act more like husband and wife. Master Hoover and Emily had lived on the ranch for many years like a married couple.

Master Hoover was delighted that Madam Charlotte took Emily's child as their son because she did what he wanted, but couldn't do because he didn't want to hurt Emily. When Emily appeared happy about Madam Charlotte taking the baby, he was surprised. That made him love Emily even more.

He started acting like a child with a new toy; he was the happiest man on earth. While he was jumping around like a little kid, the boys saw him and they were happy too.

He got busy writing an article to put in his newspaper. He thought of putting an announcement about his seventh son in the Morning Sun Newspaper, saying that his wife Madam Charlotte had given birth to her second son. That was what he wanted to do, and that is just what he did, announcing that they had named him Edward Leon Hoover.

And the deceit goes on, he thought, knowing that in a few decades no one could possibly sort it out.

Emily went in every day to breastfeed little Edward Leon. When she finished she got up to leave.

"Sit down," said Madam Charlotte one day. "We need to talk."

"Yes, Madam Charlotte." Emily sat on the bed next to her.

"I hear that slavery is going to end soon, and I am happy about that, but I will miss you and also the boys if you ever leave this place." Emily looked surprised.

"Oh, Madam Charlotte, you have no idea how much I would miss you if I ever had to leave this place. I love you so much." Emily stood, ready to return to her quarters.

Abruptly, Madam Charlotte said, "Wait a minute, Emily, I haven't finished yet. I want you to know something that I've known for quite some time about you and Master Hoover." Then she went on to say, "I know that you are lovers and that all of the boys were fathered by him."

Emily was completely surprised; she felt ashamed and speechless. Madam Charlotte continued, "I love you. I raised you like a daughter. You have been so good and attentive to my needs, and I know you love me too. For that I am thankful. Don't get me wrong. At first I was angry with both of you, but as time passed I understood. I knew that Master Hoover didn't love me. We were best friends when we were youths, and he told me everything about the girl from Chicago back then." Emily wanted to say something, but Madam kept on talking. "A girl that he described to me as a light-skinned colored girl, that girl could have been you, Emily."

Madam Charlotte went on to say, "I think I knew

it when he first brought you here, but I loved you too. You were so cute and innocent. I knew in my heart keeping you and taking good care of you was the best way of keeping both of you forever. Master Hoover had never really made love to me before that night, when he thought he was making love to you. He doesn't know that I know that. I never told him that when he was making love to me that night, he was calling out your name."

"But Madam," said Emily. Madam just kept on talking.

"So you see, your coming into our lives helped us both have a life, without hurting each other. And you know, I feel like your sons are a part of me. They are like my grandchildren." Emily was so surprised that she began to cry.

"Don't cry. You sit here and listen to the whole story about Master Hoover and me, how my marriage was arranged, and after this you can go on and feel free to love him." She didn't know that Master Hoover had already told this story to Emily, but she wanted to hear it again from Madam.

Then she told Emily that Master Hoover had really never loved her. She told her about the $10,000 payment her father made to arrange the marriage.

"I was hoping he would fall in love with me, but he never did. He really loves you. I can tell by the way he looks at you."

Neither Madam Charlotte nor Emily knew that he was leaning against the door listening to their private conversation.

≈

Emily was speechless, but in her mind she was thinking, *All those years she knew and never said anything. She must love me as much as I love her.*

"Madam, I am so sorry," said Emily. "In the beginning I was told that I was helping you by doing whatever Master Hoover told me to do."

"Emily, you *were* helping me, and because of that we have eight wonderful sons together."

"Please, Madam Charlotte, let me finish. After a few years, I knew better. But I had fallen in love with him and couldn't stop myself. I still love him, today more than ever. Master Hoover is the only man that has treated me like a person, but I felt bad about not being able to tell you the truth. You were like a mother to me and the one person that I would never want to hurt."

Madam Charlotte knew she didn't need to ask Emily for the baby then, but she wanted to anyway, before she had already taken the baby without asking.

"I want to raise Edward Leon as my son. I want to raise him as a white child," she said.

"I would be pleased and honored to have you raise little Edward Leon as your son. You raised me and I am happy. I hope that he makes you proud of him someday. I feel that's the least that I can do for you," Emily said proudly.

"But if you ever leave this place, I want you to know that he will not be leaving with you," Madam replied.

Emily had no intention of ever leaving the ranch,

but she didn't say that to Madam. Just as she was ready to give Madam Charlotte a kiss and leave, Master Hoover walked in the door. He pretended not to have heard their conversation.

"Emily has given her son to us, to be raised as a white child," Madam Charlotte told Master Hoover. She didn't want him to continue thinking that she had taken the baby. "What do you think about raising Edward Leon as a white child?" she asked.

"I think it's a great idea, especially since we gave him my name," Master Hoover replied. Then Master Hoover said to Emily, "If you decide to do this, you can never speak of it to anyone. The secret must never come out."

"It would make me proud to know my son is being raised by both of you, but what will I tell his brothers?" asked Emily.

"The boys are so young now, the only one that might want to know more would be Clarence Allen," replied Master Hoover.

"Since he is only six years old then, maybe he will forget soon, just like the others," Emily replied.

They were all hoping that Emily's other sons would think Edward Leon was Joel Edward's brother, their uncle someday. They were too young to understand it all now.

"Just don't talk about it to him now, and don't ever talk about it to them in the future, all they need to know is that they are family. Then they will remember whatever we tell them," said Master Hoover

Emily couldn't promise that she would lie to her sons. She had made up her mind that all of her sons would know the truth about their family, but she did promise not to tell the secrets to anyone else outside the family. As they grew up, she told all of her sons, except Edward Leon Hoover, that Master Hoover was their father. Edward Leon would be raised to believe that he was the child of Madam Charlotte and Master Hoover.

"We are all still together now, and we will remain together as long as slavery is still here. If slavery is no more and you wish to stay on the ranch, this is your home forever," said Master Hoover. He also told her that through the years he had fixed it so none of her sons would ever live like colored people.

"I would be very sad if you left, because I always felt we would be together forever," said Madam Charlotte.

I stood there speechless, watching those women, and I realized they were inseparable. Madam Charlotte and Emily were two very brave and wonderful women. Emily stood up and thanked them both for all of their love and support. She then went over to her son's bed and picked him up. She held him close and kissed him. I heard her whisper to him that she would always love him and she would never leave him unless she died and went to live with God. Then she laid him back down in his little bed as Madam Charlotte watched her.

After they finished talking, Emily left and Madam Charlotte went over to the baby's bed. She picked up little Edward Leon held him close and kissed him also, whispering to him that she was always going to protect him as long as she lived.

Master Hoover left right away because he thought Emily was upset and he followed her to her quarters. I think he wanted to know if she was going to keep Madam Charlotte's secret of knowing everything about their love affair. When he got to her quarters, she was crying. He walked in and put his arms around her.

"I feel so bad about what we've done for so many years. It hurt Madam Charlotte," she said. "I'm afraid our sons may suffer for the mistakes we've made."

"No, they won't," he said. "My sons will never become slaves; I've made plans to protect all of them forever. There's only one catch, and that is you. It's up to you to make sure their secrets are kept safe forever." He promised Emily that he would always protect his sons, even in his grave.

"Oh no, those secrets won't get told to anyone outside the family," Emily promised.

He noticed that she wasn't going to tell him a word of the conversation with Madam about her knowing their secret, because Madam had asked her not to tell him. That's when he knew that she could be trusted with the master plan.

And the deceit goes on, he thought, never realizing that trying to protect his sons would be the most disastrous plan of all.

CHAPTER 7

I fell asleep again, but when I opened my eyes this time I saw my brother trying to talk to me. I was so deep into my own thoughts, I never answered. He turned and walked out of the room and I felt bad about not answering him, but I knew that if I stopped I would lose my connection back in time.

I could hear my brother talking about me to my best friend in the other room. "Let her alone," my friend said. "She is really obsessed with her past." I didn't want to listen to them, and soon I couldn't hear their voices anymore.

The Civil War had come. Master Hoover had done a good job of keeping his sons a secret from the world, protecting them, or so he thought. He made sure that all of Emily's boys could pass for white if they wanted to, not just the child he'd given his name to, Edward Leon Hoover, but all of them. His deceit was done well. Everyone in town thought his boys were white; none knew a Mulatto slave was their mother.

He had no choice but to continue the deceit when all the young men were enrolled in the Army.

"They are my sister's sons from Chattanooga, Tennessee. She passed away, and her husband was killed in a fight by outlaws. The boys had no one but me left, so I raised them along with my own two sons," he explained to the army recruiter.

Before going off to war, Joel Edward Hoover (Madam Charlotte's son) got married, and his wife became pregnant. Emily's son, Evan Lee, became a father also, naming his son Peter Joe, after his favorite brother.

The boys were sent to war. The Hoover boys were in the First Battle of Bull Run; the Confederate troops, reinforced in time, won a resounding victory. General Irvin McDowell prepared 130,000 men to challenge Lee, whose army of 60,000 was massed in Virginia near Fredericksburg. The letter arrived shortly after the battle in Virginia.

> Dear Mr. Hoover,
>
> We regret being the bearer of this news about your sister's sons. They were killed in Battle in Virginia. Peter Joe Allen, Willie Leroy Allen, and David Roy Allen have died bravely; we pray they rest in peace. There is some good news. We are happy to inform you that your sister's son Joel Jon Allen, who was found wounded, is alive, and will be home soon.
>
> Regretfully,
>
> Confederate Army

~

Below the signature was a postscript.

Just in today—

While writing you this letter, we regret this notation regarding your firstborn son, Mr. Hoover. Your son Joel Edward was also killed in battle. It was just one day after his cousins. Just today the list of the soldiers killed in battle was made available, and your son's name appeared on the list of casualties.

The news was so painful; it knocked Master Hoover off his feet. Lee lost nearly one-fifth of his men and his brilliant general, Stonewall Jackson. Master Hoover lost his only white son, and three sons by the woman he loved. He cried like a baby when they got the news.

It is my fault, he thought. *I am responsible for all four of my Allen boys getting in the armed forces, with all my lies and secrets.* He'd enlisted Emily's boys but Charlotte's son Joel Edward didn't have to go to war, because he was her only son. It was his decision to go, to join in the fight for justice.

This news almost killed Master Hoover. He started to get weaker and weaker as the days went by. Master Hoover and Madam Charlotte, although elderly, were doing well. Emily was getting older too, and taking care of them both. After they got the news about the boys, they all seemed to deteriorate. They were heartbroken and speechless for months.

Emily wandered around the ranch alone, looking

~

at the horses, not wanting the others to see the pain in her face. The boys liked the horses.

Her son Joey Jon was still in the Army. She had fears about him being killed also. The Army had said in the letter that he was coming home soon. Emily still couldn't face the fact that three sons were dead, and she was afraid to feel happy about Joey Jon because she feared it would cause him to die too.

Emily couldn't smile until one day Joel Jon, his wife, and their new baby girl showed up at the door. She looked up at her son's beautiful face, and lit up like a Christmas tree. In all this pain, she was happier than she had ever been.

His wife, Jacqueline, who was white, was completely aware of his ethnicity. Emily, who had never seen her granddaughter before, was thrilled to find out they'd named the baby after her. She loved little Emily the instant she saw her.

During that time Master Hoover became very sick. The loss of his sons devastated him.

More of my childhood memories were coming back: I remembered what Big Daddy said about him.

"A man that was so strong just fell apart overnight," he'd said while reminiscing about family stories while I sat near him on the porch.

Master Hoover couldn't stop thinking about how he had lied to get his sons into the Army. He thought about the men he was involved with in the HMC Club, who took the lives of innocent people just because they were different. He knew

~

the seeds that he had planted in his life were now growing back into the lives of his loved ones. He never understood that old saying, "You reap what you sow," until now.

"If only I'd told the truth," he kept repeating to himself. Then he thought, *I used my best friend to help get those boys into the Confederate Army, lying to them. Telling them my sons were my sister's children, just to get them accepted as white men.*

He had promised Emily that their sons would never live like slaves and he would protect them forever. He even lied to his sons and he never got a chance to tell them the truth. These tragedies left Master Hoover, Madam Charlotte, and Emily heartbroken for many years. It was said that Master Hoover never really recovered from it.

I found myself sleepy again. In no time the war was over. "The war is over, we are free, we are free at last!" People were shouting and running in the street.

I looked around and everyone was all dressed up; they looked like they were going on a trip or moving to a new place. People were running around, crowds of people were all over the place and I wondered where they had all come from. I had never seen so much excitement in the streets before.

The only sons still alive were Clarence Allen, Evan Lee Allen, Joey Jon Allen, and Edward Leon Hoover. They found a way, through the strength of Emily, to go on into the future carrying the pain of a family lost at war.

CHAPTER 8

I walked around looking for something that showed the date. I looked on the table and saw a newspaper. Just as I ran over to look, I saw Emily's son, Clarence Allen, picked it up. He began reading to Miss Lilly. The war had ended and the slaves were freed, but the pain would not end so quickly.

"Over 600,000 people have been killed," he read. "And even more were wounded." A haunted look entered his eyes. "I really miss my brothers, David Roy, Peter Joe, Willie Leroy, and Madam's Joel." Clarence Allen finally said to Rosa that it was 1865. He still felt a deep sadness. He started naming off the loved ones and friends who had been lost in the war. "I'm glad it's over," he said finally.

After slavery, the Hoovers had given their freed slaves the homes where they were living in exchange for continuing to work on the plantation. Each family had separate little huts on the plantation, with two rooms and a kitchen. No stove or ice box. They used buckets with blocks of ice to keep their milk and butter cool.

I had drifted off again. Opening my eyes again, I started looking for Emily or anyone that I knew.

When I saw the ranch I ran over to Miss Lilly's and looked in the door. *She looks about ninety years old*, I thought.

Miss Lilly looked so lonely. I looked for her husband Willie, but he was not there. She was sitting in the big rocking chair reading the paper. Miss Lilly and Willie now had a nice two-bedroom house on the plantation, built just for them. They practically ran the plantation, and were like family to the Hoovers, who had come to trust and need Willie and Miss Lilly.

Suddenly I saw two people coming into the room from the kitchen. I realized it must be Emily's first son Clarence Allen and his wife Rosa, who was Miss Lilly's daughter. I saw a young man, and thought he was their son.

"Hello, Peter Joe," Clarence Allen and Rosa said. I realized it was Evan Lee's son, named after his brother who had died in the war.

Peter Joe, I thought. *What a nice friendly name. I wish I could get to know him.* His father, Evan Lee, was close to his brothers, but he was especially close to his brother Peter Joe. Evan Lee had been sick a lot when they were growing up, so he couldn't always do his chores. Peter Joe would look after him and help Evan Lee finish his chores. Peter Joe even got in trouble for Evan Lee with Master Hoover one day, and took his punishment. Evan Lee never forgot that, and when his son was born, he named him after his brother. He came home on leave once, before he was killed, and

~

got a chance to meet Little Peter Joe. He was so proud of little Peter Joe, his namesake.

Clarence Allen felt like reminiscing with his wife Rosa about the past. She knew about a lot of the story because she had known the family her entire life. Although she was with him during this time, I don't think she knew the details of some family secrets. Rosa and I were ready, sitting there listening to him tell the story, only she didn't know that I was on the floor next to her listening too.

"Well, this is my memories. Mama Emily couldn't rest late one night and she went into Master Hoover's room to check on him, when she found him not feeling well. She decided to give him his morning bath, hoping that it would make him feel better. She noticed that while she was bathing him, he was falling asleep right in the middle of his bath. Mama Emily knew that wasn't like him, because he still enjoyed her touch, even though he was an old man. She knew he would never go to sleep while she was touching his body. His body was very warm." Clarence Allen remembered that she had called him, very concerned.

"Clarence can you come here right away?" she yelled. I ran in as fast as I could to see what was going on.

"Is something wrong?" I asked.

"Yes, I think so. Master Hoover seemed very weak while taking his bath, and he may have a fever."

I'd noticed that Master Hoover was weak, but thought it was because he was up in his nineties.

≈

He was ninety-seven to be exact, and hadn't been able to get out of bed on his own for two years now. Mama Emily was trying to take care of running the house and everyone else. I worried about her health. After all, Mama Emily was seventy-two years old herself.

I was fifty-one myself, and I wanted to help. But she still tried to do everything herself. Madam Charlotte was eighty-eight years old, and everyone was surprised that she had lived that long because of her rare blood disease. Mama Emily was not ready to let go of either one of them. So for years she made sure that they ate well, and had their regular doctor's visits.

I could hear Mama Emily calling one of us to come with the carriage, because it was time to get the doctor for Master Hoover. Mama Emily always called him Edward or Master. We all knew the truth by now because Mama Emily had told us, but they never told the boys that were killed in the war. All three died without knowing the truth. They also never told Edward Leon Hoover, Mama's seventh son, the one she gave to Madam.

Master Hoover didn't want to tell Edward Leon the truth about his mixed blood. The boys were all told about Mama Emily being a nanny for the big house. Edward Leon Hoover was told that Emily was his father's bed warmer only when he was older, and even then Master Hoover didn't tell him Emily was his mother. When the boys were small, he told them she was his sister, and later he told them another lie. Master Hoover lied so much, until his sons didn't know what to believe.

～

Mama Emily told her boys the truth when the Civil War ended, except for Edward Leon, because he was passing for white. Master Hoover still didn't want to tell the truth on his sick bed. He always said he was going to tell Edward Leon the truth after the war was over. But he never did. He told so many other lies, and we were forbidden to tell Edward Leon about the secrets.

So, now that Master Hoover was on his sickbed and might die, it looked like he was going to take the secrets to his grave without telling the only son that was carrying the family name.

I thought that if he kept those secrets from Edward Leon, it was going to be a curse on both the Allens and the Hoovers. That didn't matter to him. Keeping his family white was more important than worrying about a family curse.

I always knew why my father liked to call himself "The Master of Deceit." Madam Charlotte even wanted to tell Edward Leon the truth, but Master Hoover forbade her to.

While I was growing up, I watched my mother looking after Edward Leon around the clock every day, and every night. Mama Emily acted just like a real daughter to Madam, and just like a real wife to Master Hoover. She had been taking care of them for so many years, nobody believed she was anything but part of the Hoovers, and she looked white. So Mama Emily had a good chance of living as a white lady all of her life, and she did.

People in the community knew she took care of Madam Charlotte and the Master. Some were told that she was Master Hoover's sister, and others were told she was his daughter. No one really cared who she was, just what she was—black or white?

I watched Mama Emily going in and out of Master Hoover's room that day after his bath.

"Son, go into town quickly and fetch me the doctor because Master Hoover is burning up with fever and I can't get it down," she said.

So I ran out to the barn and got the carriage. I saw Evan Lee fixing one of the horse's shoes. Evan Lee was the caretaker for the horses, now that old Willie had gone to meet his maker. When I told him about the emergency, he jumped in the carriage and off we went.

While we were gone, Mama Emily worked to get the fever down but had no luck. When we returned she was almost in tears. She was sitting in a chair next to his bed with her head down, praying for the man she loved.

Rosa and I were really enjoying Clarence Allen's storytelling. He went on.

When we arrived with the doctor and walked into the room, Mama Emily ran to Dr. Pitts to tell him that Master Hoover was very ill. Even though Dr. Pitts was quite old and retired by now, he was still the best doctor in town.

"Don't worry about Master Hoover, this old fox is not ready to go yet." Dr. Pitts said. He went to the bed to examine Master Hoover. He'd come prepared and brought medicine for Master's high fever. After finishing his examination and giving him the medicine, he decided to sit with him and wait. Master Hoover never stirred for two hours; then he awoke. His fever had gone down. Dr. Pitts waited another hour, sitting with family at Master Hoover's bedside. Emily was in the room the whole time.

I wondered what Madam Charlotte thought about being left out of the room from her husband, until I found out from her myself. I asked her if she wanted me to help her into Master's room. I only did that because I thought she felt bad.

Madam Charlotte answered, "I'm doing all right, son, and Emily is the one that should be in the room with him now anyway."

Then she told me she couldn't help him now anyway because she was too old. Their daughter Emily was doing a good job taking care of them both.

After waiting another hour, Dr. Pitts fell asleep and Emily prayed.

"Hello there, beautiful." Hearing the voice, she looked up, and it was Master Hoover trying to sit up in bed and that woke up the doctor.

"Hello there, you old fox," said Dr. Pitts.

"I wasn't talking to you! You old goat," answered Master Hoover. They all laughed, but Master Hoover felt pain in his chest and had to lie back in bed.

Dr. Pitts examined him again, when suddenly Master Hoover really started to have trouble breathing. Emily was afraid and began to cry.

"Get your sons right away, Emily," said Dr. Pitts.

Emily ran out to fetch her sons, and in moments

we were all in the room together.

"Take your mother out and keep her there until I come see you," said Dr. Pitts to Evan Lee.

The doctor knew Master Hoover was having a heart attack and he was trying to keep Emily from getting too upset, and was hoping he could get it under some kind of control.

"Clarence Allen, help me lift him, we need to get him into a sitting position so he can get some air." Dr. Pitts said.

He gave him some medicine to make Master Hoover relax. After the doctor got control of the situation, he waited with me for half an hour. Master Hoover was resting comfortably, and he went back to sleep.

When Dr. Pitts came out of the room he could tell that Emily was frightened. He knew that he had to tell her the truth.

"Master Hoover had a heart attack and he is resting. You need to start calling all of the family members who are away because he may only be with us another two weeks, and that's putting it generously because he is very weak now." he said.

Emily stood, dazed. Madam and the others were terribly sad.

"I'll get in touch with the others for you Mama Emily," I told her.

At that time Rosa and I, her mother Miss Lilly, Evan Lee, his wife Elaine, their son Peter Joe, Pastor Martin, his wife Sister Harriet, and their two sons John and David Martin were already here. Our friends from other plantations who wanted to share was welcome to come on Sundays to the large church we'd built to praise the Lord. The pastor was well known in the community as a great speaker, and his wife Harriet could sing the gospel like nobody else. If times were different, she'd have traveled the world singing gospel songs. Pastor and Harriet Martin could have left Hoover Ranch any time they wanted, with the end of slavery. Since Sister Harriet had started the children's choir, which they called "The Divine Healing Ministry," she didn't want to leave them. She traveled with the children's choir all around the area, visiting with other community youth groups.

Emily went over to Madam Charlotte and put her arms around her.

"Now sweetheart, you knew this was coming, and you need to be strong for me because my time is coming soon also," said Madam Charlotte.

"Mother, what's wrong? Are you all right?" Emily asked.

"I'm fine, but I'm an old woman now," Madam Charlotte replied. "Now, you must listen to me. Master Hoover and I have loved you since the day we met. Now I need your help." She paused. "There is something very important that I must tell Edward before he dies, and you must be strong for the rest of us."

"I'll be strong for you, Mother, I'll always love the both of you," said Emily.

"Okay, sweetheart! Now, Emily, this is what we are going to do. Whenever he wakes up, I want you to go in with him and tell him your goodbyes. Then I want you to tell him that I want to see him alone, to say my own good-bye to him." Emily wondered what Madam Charlotte had on her mind because she was acting so secretive.

Dr. Pitts didn't leave, he just went over to the corner where Master Hoover kept his big rocking chair, and went to sleep. Emily went to sit with Master Hoover until he awakened. She did exactly what Madam told her. Madam Charlotte wanted to make sure Master Hoover didn't die before she had her say with him.

When I came back into the room, I told my grandmother that I had sent messages to everyone who lived in the states. I'd sent messages to all the family in California, Washington, D.C., and Chicago. Edward Leon Hoover, who lived in Washington, D.C., told me he would send telegrams to the others who were out of the country. Madam Charlotte seemed pleased with what I had done.

'Master Hoover is awake, and he's asking to see the doctor alone.' Emily said. Evan Lee went over to the big chair and awakened the doctor.

The doctor went into the room and closed the door behind him. Master Hoover wanted to know from the doctor if he was dying. "Why is my chest in so much pain? It's hurting so much I can hardly breathe," he asked.

"You've had a heart attack," Dr. Pitts told him.

"Am I getting ready to die? How long do I have?"

"My old friend, you're not doing so well," said Dr. Pitts gently, and continued, "I must tell you that another heart attack could come at any time."

~

"You old goat, you better keep your hands off Emily when I'm gone, I know you've been wanting to for a long time," said Master Hoover to his old friend.

Dr. Pitts laughed, and said, "Edward, you've been a lucky man, you old fox, having two such beautiful and wonderful women in your life." He shook his head, then continued, "You listen here, don't you worry about Emily, she don't love nor want any man but you, you lucky dog."

"All right now, that's enough. How long do I have?" Master asked.

"Well Ed, maybe two weeks, and maybe more, but that's putting it out there," Dr. Pitts said.

"Listen you old goat, don't you leave this house until I check out, you hear?"

"I'm not going anywhere. Look here, I plan to stay awhile," said Dr. Pitts.

"On your way out, tell Emily to come in. I'll see you in the morning," said Master Hoover."

Clarence Allen had a way of storytelling like my Big Daddy, and my spirit loved listening to him. I made myself comfortable to hear him go on.

Dr. Pitts walked into the other room and found Madam Charlotte talking to Emily.

"Edward wants you, Emily," he said.

She looked into the old doctor's eyes, hoping to find some kind of hope for her lover, but all Emily saw was death. She got up slowly and sadly, and as she walked toward Master Hoover's door, she looked back at Madam.

"Be strong, Emily," Madam Charlotte said.

She waved her on into the room. Madam Charlotte knew the pain that Emily would face soon enough. Her lover Percy Carson had passed away two years earlier.

As Emily entered the room Master Hoover was sitting up in bed with two pillows behind his back. He looked toward the door, and saw her standing there.

"Hello! Sweetheart, come on over here closer to me and don't be afraid," he said.

Emily looked at him for a moment, thinking how wonderful he looked. He didn't seem to be sick or dying. She walked over to him and laid her head on his chest. He hugged her very tightly in his arms.

"How about giving this old man a bath?" he asked. He always liked her touch, even at ninety-eight years old.

"Edward I would like to give you a bath, but only if you promise to behave," said Emily.

"How would an old goat like me misbehave?" Master Hoover smiled at Emily, and she smiled back.

"Try not to get too excited. Remember your heart—I don't want to lose you yet," Emily said.

"Oh, sweetheart, I don't want to ever leave you, but I know I must. I am taking you with me in my heart and I will be waiting for you for all eternity."

"Master, you know I don't like that kind of talk. I don't want you leaving me. If you must go, you know that I'll always love you and keep you alive in my heart." She leaned closer to him, fighting tears.

"I will come to you one day, my love."

They held each other for a moment and then Emily, with tears in her eyes, went into the bathroom to get his bath ready. As she filled the wash pan with warm water, he had tears in his eyes also. Tenderly, she began to bathe him. Emily washed him all over with very warm water, and a soft cloth.

"I still enjoy the touch of your soft hands. I wish old bud down there would do what it used to do when you touch it. I wish I could have you just one more time," he said.

"I love you too, but I don't want you getting one bit excited, so calm down or I will let Dr. Pitts come in here and bathe you."

Well, Master Hoover laughed at that.

"I would surely die if that old codger tried to bathe me, but if I died right at this moment with your hands touching me, I would say what a way to go." They both smiled.

Emily finished his bath. "Now, Emily, would you tell Madam Charlotte to come talk to me, because I have some things I need to talk over with her," he said.

Emily agreed. "She asked if you would see her because she also has things to talk over with you."

Emily hugged and kissed him and turned to walk out of the room. When she got to the door, she looked back at him just lying in bed. He looked good to her, not like a sick man at all. *He can't be dying*, she told herself.

I thought my Big Daddy could tell stories well, but Clarence Allen had him beat. Well, after all, he probably taught my Big Daddy. Clarence Allen told the story so well that soon, we didn't even notice him talking. It seemed like we were there, inside his story.

CHAPTER 9

Emily came to Madam Charlotte.

"Master Hoover is asking for you," she said.

When she entered his room, Master Hoover was sitting up and looking like the picture of health. Madam Charlotte put her arms around him.

"You're looking much better," she said.

"Thank you, Charlotte. I asked to see you because I have something to say to you before I check out of here," he said quietly.

"That's good, I'm here to listen, and I also have something that I need to tell you," she said gently.

"My dear Charlotte, I'm so sorry that I was not able to be the husband you deserved." His eyes were moist. "I'm asking your forgiveness for hurting you all these years." When he finished Madam Charlotte had tears in her eyes.

"Well Edward, at least your dream came true." She looked into his eyes, and said, "I didn't want you to get away from me either, before asking you to forgive me too. I have also hurt you for many years."

Master Hoover may have been sick but he still had a good memory. "Charlotte, what in the devil

192 · *Millie L. McGhee*

are you talking about? Are you talking about Emily?"
he asked.

"No, Edward, I am not talking about Emily.
Remember when we were kids, and we were best
friends? You told me about the half-white colored
girl in Chicago? You were away at boarding school."

"Yes, I remember."

"Well, when you told me about her it was the
same day that our fathers arranged our marriage."

"Yes, go on, so what?" He sounded a little impatient.

"Okay! Stop interrupting me and please just listen." Charlotte went on to say, "I was in love with
you for the longest time when we were children,
but I was afraid to tell you for fear of losing my best
friend forever. That's when I knew I could never tell
you my feelings, as I got older I fell in love with
Percy. After you told me about the girl that you
loved—I will never forget your words, you said, 'I
will never love any girl, but her.' I knew then I had
lost you forever as a lover. We were still best friends,
so I settled for that, and I decided we would be best
friends forever.

"But you said, 'I don't want to marry you, Charlotte, because you are my best friend. Friends don't
marry best friends, unless they are in love, and we are
not in love.' Remember, I asked you why not? And you
answered, 'Because I want to have a best friend forever.' And that's when I told you that I had an idea."

He smiled gently. Charlotte had always been a
dear friend to him.

≈

"This idea," she continued. "I would help you have the girl of your dreams and keep your best friend at the same time. I felt that I had lost Percy Carson, my lover, forever, so I was going to settle for a life with my best friend with no romance. Maybe in my head I was hoping you'd fall in love with me, but either way, I wanted to marry you.

"'Let's play a game with our parents and trick them,' I told you, "Do you remember that?" she asked.

"I remember that day very well," said Master Hoover.

"Well, I told you we could pretend to be married just to keep your father from taking away your inheritance, and then you could go and get your girl from Chicago."

"I remember you telling me about an idea you had, but I'm not clear anymore about the rest of the conversation." He wanted her to get to the point. "Madam Charlotte, what are you trying to tell me?" he asked.

"Emily has been your dream for years, and I've known about you two almost from the beginning."

Master Hoover wasn't surprised and was too tired to act like he was. He'd overheard her telling Emily that she knew many years ago. She still had to tell him the most important part, so she spoke a little faster.

"All I'm asking, as your best friend, is that you listen to everything I'm trying to tell you. Remember after our marriage we all signed a marriage certificate at father's house, and I was supposed to take it to the Marshall's office the next day for filing?" she asked.

"Yes, I remember," he replied.

She pulled their marriage certificate out of her pocket. She gave the certificate to him. It should have had a stamp confirming the marriage, but he noticed that it had not been registered.

"What is this Charlotte?" he asked.

"Our arranged marriage was a pretend marriage all those years! Look at it, I never filed it," said Charlotte.

Master Hoover really was shocked now. He'd been single all his life, and never even knew it. The only woman he'd ever really wanted to marry was Emily. And he could have! He felt sad, and wondered if this was Charlotte's way of hurting him for all the lies and deceit he'd subjected her to during their long pretend marriage.

Does she want to get her revenge, now that I'm on my deathbed? he wondered. *If so, it's working*, he thought. Knowing that he could have married Emily hurt him badly. *All my sons could have been given my name*, he thought. *Of course, I deserved what she did to me for all the bad things I did to her.* He was determined not to be angry with her. Besides, he wanted her to forgive him.

"When you brought Emily to the ranch I decided never to file that certificate, because I saw that girl you loved years ago in Emily," said Charlotte.

Master Hoover was overwhelmed by what she had just told him.

～

"Edward, you should marry Emily before you die, and make everything right with God."

My soul could be saved after all? he questioned to himself when he heard Madam Charlotte's plan.

"You know I would love to marry Emily, but if it will hurt you in any way I will not," he said.

'I wouldn't be alive if it wasn't for Emily," said Madam Charlotte. "For years, it seems like you and Emily were married anyway. Now I'm sorry I didn't forgive you sooner," she said.

"I could only dream about this, and before I die it will actually happen," said Master Hoover.

"Lord knows Emily deserves happiness," said Madam Charlotte.

Madam Charlotte and Master Hoover decided to surprise Emily by holding a secret, private marriage ceremony. They only wanted family there, but Dr. Pitts was considered family so he was invited.

Madam Charlotte had to let Rosa and Miss Lilly in on the secret because she needed their help planning the wedding. There wasn't much time, so he gave them just three days.

Master Hoover began to feel better. Happiness motivated him to fight for his life, but he was still in trouble and his heart remained weak. The next day Emily came to give him his morning bath. He was smiling, and sitting up in bed reading a romantic novel called, *How to Love Forever.*

Emily had seen Madam Charlotte emerge from her talk with Master Hoover the day before, in a

196 · *Millie L. McGhee*

cheerful mood. *They must have confessed everything and forgave each other, there are no more secrets between them*, thought Emily.

Emily had prayed to God for years, asking his forgiveness for having children with another woman's husband.

"Come, Emily, give me a kiss," he beckoned.

"Master Hoover, what's going on? What happened between you and Madam?"

"Stop calling me 'Master.'" He took her hand. "Emily, please forgive me for not telling you to stop calling me that a long time ago."

She looked uncertain, wondering what happened between him and Madam Charlotte.

"Nothing happened between Charlotte and I, we just forgave each other for the wrongdoing we did, and the pain we caused each other. And I must say, that made me feel free and wonderful."

"Master—I mean Edward—I want to be forgiven too, for all the things that I did to cause this to happen between us, because I loved you from the beginning." She had wanted to confess her sins to God, so she asked, "I wonder, would you be with me when I confess to Pastor Martin?"

"I'd love to, if I can get out of bed," said Master Hoover.

"If it's all right with you, Pastor Martin will come to the house to see us," she said.

"Fine! That's fine. I have some questions to ask Pastor Martin myself."

Nothing could have worked out better. Miss Lilly and Rosa were wondering how they could get Pastor Martin into Master's room with Emily, without her figuring out they were up to something.

Two days later everything was in place. The pastor and his wife knew it was a surprise wedding; they already had the marriage certificate.

Emily Allen and Master Hoover would finally join as husband and wife, after fifty-eight years of love and having seven sons together. Madam Charlotte was glad she was still there to see it. All the family members arrived from different cities, thinking they were coming for a funeral.

The family was all caught up in the wedding, and had forgotten about Master Hoover dying. They even forgot that the family members coming from out of town thought it was to see Master Hoover before he died.

We saw the carriage coming toward the house from town. It was Madam Charlotte's daughter-in-law, Eva, and Eva's daughter, Charlotte, from California.

Mama Emily sent me and Evan Lee back and forth to the train station in the horse carriage, picking up family members.

Eva brought her seven-year-old daughter and only child by Joel Edward Hoover, Madam's only son. He died before he even had a chance to see his daughter. The Hoovers from Washington, D.C. came also. Edward Leon Hoover and his wife, Sheila Mae, brought their son Edward Earl Hoover, his wife, Carol, and son, J.E. The only ones that still lived on Hoover Ranch were myself and my wife Rosa Carson Allen; her eighty-five-year-old mother, Miss Lilly; and Evan Lee, his wife, Elaine, and their son, Peter Joe. Out back in the slave quarters were Pastor John Martin, his wife Sister Harriet, and their sons John Junior and David Martin.

They were all there just in time for a wedding that they didn't know was scheduled. Rosa was trying to keep the wedding a secret. Miss Lilly tried to tell each couple as they walked through the door. It seemed to be great news to everyone except Edward Leon Hoover, who still didn't know the truth about Emily.

Edward Leon Hoover thought Emily was his nanny, and there were other lies that his father had told him. He didn't know what to believe. Even though he loved Emily, he didn't want to be colored. He had lived his entire life as a white man. He was angry with his father for doing what he thought was shameful for a white man to do, and that was choosing a slave woman to love.

"I came only out of respect for my mother Charlotte, who is losing Master Hoover," he said. "I know they didn't live their lives as a married couple because of my father's love affair with Mama Emily."

He was teaching his son, Edward Earl, not to associate himself with colored people, and he didn't know he was a colored man himself. Everyone just listened to him and said nothing to him.

In the meantime, Madam and Emily were in the

other room very happy working on another family secret.

"Emily, I'm going to ask you to wear my wedding dress to Master's confession party," said Madam Charlotte.

That was the lie they told Emily. Madam Charlotte didn't want Master Hoover to see Emily on her wedding day, or before the wedding, and contrived a reason for Emily to give him his bath the night before.

Edward Leon went to see Madam Charlotte on the morning of the wedding.

"Can't you stop this madness? It's indecent," he said, but it didn't help him.

"No one is going to interfere with this marriage while I'm in this house, one day you might understand. Or you might not. That's up to you," she said.

Miss Lilly, Rosa, and Madam Charlotte all helped to dress Emily for the surprise of her life. My brothers and I, except Edward Leon, made a big to-do over Master Hoover, dressing him in his best suit and putting him in his rolling chair. They pushed him into the big party room of the church. Everyone came all dressed in their Sunday best for a big family celebration.

Emily was proud that Master Hoover was ready to ask God for forgiveness. She felt like God had answered her prayers. For many years, Emily had prayed for Master Hoover to ask God's forgiveness before he died. At last, he was coming to Christ, and his whole family was attending the church service to welcome him. Or so she thought.

As the ceremony began, the guests were seated in the pews, light shining in from the windows. The pastor and his family were waiting.

It was eleven in the morning, and they had chairs on both sides of Master Hoover's chair, waiting for his ladies. The crowd hushed as Madam Charlotte, his lifetime best friend, and Emily, the woman he loved for nearly sixty years, came into the room. They walked in together, holding each other's arms, as mother and daughter.

Emily wore Madam's wedding dress, with lovely white flowers in her beautiful hair. Madam Charlotte wore a pretty, beige satin dress trimmed in lace with attractive white flowers in her hair also. The pastor stood up.

"Let us all prepare for prayer, to bless this fellowship," he said.

After the prayer he turned the meeting over to Master Hoover, sitting in a rolling chair all dressed in his best. His sons all, even Edward stood with him. The boys pushed him up to the front of the room to speak to his family.

"To my family members and friends: I am weak and not in the best of health, but I am the happiest man on earth today." He coughed slightly and continued. "I am leaving you all sooner than you think, and I hope you can forgive me if I have hurt any of you in the past. It is a wonderful day to be with all of you. I want you to know that what I did during my lifetime was out of love for my family. My wish is that you will all continue to protect this family, as I did." He paused then said, "What you are about to witness here today is a private family affair, not to be repeated to anyone outside this family."

He was getting weak, but he wanted to finish what he was saying.

"When I am gone I am asking you not to be sad for me, I want you to have a celebration instead." He looked at the pastor. "I am ready to start."

Everybody turned and looked at Emily. She looked behind her to see what everybody was staring at, and the pastor prepared to make the wedding announcement to her, since everyone else knew.

"Dearly beloved, we are gathered here to witness the marriage of two great people, Master Edward D. Hoover to the love of his life Emily Allen."

Emily looked at Madam Charlotte, thinking, *What is going on? Marriage? They must have kept this a secret!* Master Hoover looked at Emily's face. His heart nearly stopped just because of her beauty, and they say he got excited. The moment had come to ask for God's blessing upon their union.

The pastor began. "Emily, would you stand and come forward with your mother?"

Emily thought she was escorting Madam to be remarried, because she couldn't believe this was her wedding day. When she got to the altar, they planned to bring Emily and Master Hoover together for their vows.

"Step up here," the pastor motioned to Emily.

~

Just at that moment, Master Hoover passed out. Shock overtook the church. Everybody stood up at once. Master Hoover's sons, the Pastor, and Dr. Pitts rushed to his side, but they could not rouse him. The doctor checked him.

"Carry your father back to bed right away," he said to his sons.

Madam Charlotte was devastated.

Stunned with disbelief, Emily looked at Madam Charlotte, tears streaming from her eyes.

"He wanted to ask God's forgiveness. Why now?" Emily asked.

Tears rolled down her face, and spilled from Madam Charlotte's eyes too, as they held each other. They were crying, but not for the same reasons.

"Master Hoover's last words were for us to celebrate his going, and not to be sad, so you may start to celebrate now," the pastor said, as he left the room with his wife to join the doctor.

"Is he dead?" everyone was whispering by now. Emily and Madam Charlotte did not move, holding each other's hand.

Edward Leon and his family didn't want to admit they were happy that it didn't happen, but they were. They hoped this event would never be talked about again, and they were angry at Edward Leon's father for even thinking about marrying a nigger. Half-white or not, Emily was still a nigger to them.

Emily and Madam Charlotte struggled to their feet, barely able to see as they walked together to be with Master Hoover. They both had eyes filled with tears.

~

"He is at peace now. He asked for forgiveness and that saved him," said Madam

Emily knew he'd asked her not to be sad, so she tried, but she felt such a sense of loss it took her breath away.

The door to Master Hoover's room opened, and his sons came out; with the exception of Edward Leon, they all went directly to Emily to comfort her.

"It was another heart attack," her son Evan Lee told her, holding her small hand in his big strong one.

The Pastor and Dr. Pitts stood by Master Hoover's bed.

"Do you think he's going to make it?" the pastor whispered to Dr. Pitts.

Just as Dr. Pitts prepared to answer, Master Hoover opened his eyes. Remembering that it was his wedding day, he tried to get up.

"Lay still. Don't you move," the doctor ordered.

"You had another heart attack. Any more excitement will kill you." He told him.

The doctor knew that surviving even one more day was unlikely, even with rest. To keep him sedated, he prepared a shot of whiskey. Master Hoover moved his lips. They leaned toward him to hear what he was trying to say.

"I want to talk to Pastor first," he said very softly.

Pastor Martin pulled a chair close to the bed, sitting very near so he wouldn't need to talk very loud.

"Pastor, do you think your God would listen to me now?" He asked.

204 · Millie L. McGhee

"God is not just my God, He is everyone's God, and if you want Him in your heart, all you have to do is invite Him in. He is always listening," the pastor said.

"What should I say?" asked Master Hoover feebly.

"Just open your heart and let Him in." To everyone's astonishment, Master Hoover began to take off his shirt to show his chest. The pastor's wife turned away quickly to avoid seeing him exposed. Master Hoover noticed her turning away.

"Well now, Sister Harriet, I have lots of respect for God's leaders, and I ain't never tried to do nothing with you, nor would I ever do something improper in front of you," he said.

After taking off his shirt, he was ready to talk to God.

"God, Pastor told me to open up my heart to you now, and I want you to see my chest to prove that my heart is opened." Sister Harriet started to smile at him, so he stopped speaking to God for a moment to say a few words to her.

"That's better, Sister Harriet, because the only woman I ever exposed myself to was Emily, and now she is my wife. I know I didn't get a chance to marry her in the eyes of all of my children yet." He pointed to the pastor. "Pastor, get me those papers. I want to sign them right now before I go." As the pastor handed Master Hoover the papers to sign, he went right on talking. "Sister Harriet, come on over closer to me now. I want you to give this certificate of marriage to my best friend Charlotte. She will know what to do."

"I'd be happy to do that for you, Master Hoover," Sister Harriet said, and she did.

He then looked at the pastor and continued his talk with God. "Well, God here is my heart," he said, patting his chest. "Come on in now and save my old soul, but first I want to tell you something: I did do one or two good things in my life. I always took good care of Charlotte, even though she tells me now that we weren't married, and I never tried to have sex with her because I loved Emily. The only sex we had was her doing, and it wasn't mine." He stopped and thought for a moment, then continued.

"The only woman I ever really wanted was Emily, and I wished I had married her, but you know, I married her in my heart, God. The last thing I want to say is, you know I didn't think of them as slaves. I loved my slaves, and I was good to them." When he finished opening his heart to God, he looked at the pastor. "Do you think He heard me?" he asked.

"God would have heard you if you just thought the words in your mind," said the pastor. That was surprising to the master.

"Well then, he knows more about my heart than I thought," he said finally.

Dr. Pitts was listening, and he wondered what Master Hoover meant when he said that to God.

"That must account for my longevity. God must have given it to me."

～

The pastor nodded his head. "How are you feeling after your confession?" the pastor asked.

"My soul is happy, but my chest feels like a ton of bricks is sitting on top of it. I just want some peace from this pain now."

Sister Harriet walked over to comfort him. "Master Hoover, I would like to sing a song for you, if that would make you feel better."

He smiled and said, "I thought you'd never ask." He relaxed in the spirit to listen to the song.

She chose the perfect song for him. She sang "Peace in the Valley" in a voice so rich it could have been a full choir. Everyone in the house was spellbound. The pastor prayed for the soul of Master Hoover. Silently, gently, he reached over with his finger and closed Master Hoover's eyes. Master Hoover had gone to the other side.

"I'm going out to tell the family that the old fox, and my dear friend, is gone," said Dr. Pitts.

They already knew. They heard his soul depart in Sister Harriet's song. As her voice filled the air, they had stood spellbound. It was as if his spirit came to each of them to say good-bye.

When the doctor came out of the Master's room, everyone was standing near the door as quiet as a mouse.

"He's gone home," he simply said.

Emily and Madam Charlotte clung to each other in their pain, remembering his request. *Don't be sad for me*, he'd said.

~

They all tried. To honor him, they had a celebration when they laid him to rest, one of the biggest celebrations ever on Hoover's Ranch. They held it in the church that Master Hoover built. Sister Harriet sang, uplifting everyone with her lovely voice.

It seemed that everyone present could feel Master Hoover's acceptance of this celebration in the spirit in the church. He had to be smiling. Emily and even Madam Charlotte were dancing with him in spirit. It was a glorious home going.

And with that, Clarence Allen ended his story. I cried, listening to the story, hearing Sister Harriet's song in my mind. I sensed that Master Hoover was at peace.

I needed to go back to the future, but this was so interesting. When Clarence Allen finished telling us the story not one person's eyes were dry. Rosa reached out and hugged him, and so did I, only he didn't know it. At least, I thought he didn't, but he said something strange.

"Thank you, Rosa." He paused. "Rosa, I felt my father hugging me too. I felt something touching my hands when I was hugging you."

Then I knew it was time to get home to the future. But before I went, I saw him put his arms around Rosa.

"Look how many family members are gone," he said quietly. "My dad, good old Willie, Harry, and

Sweet Anna. Then the Civil War took Peter Joe, Willie Leroy, David Roy, and Joel Edward."

I found myself missing Mama Emily and Madam Charlotte, and I knew I couldn't go back yet. I wanted to see if they were lonely, because they had lost so many loved ones. The older they got, the more they missed the people they lost.

The oldest still living was Miss Lilly. She still had her good memory and still guided the younger folks. The young people always looked up to the eldest, and everyone looked up to Miss Lilly and took good care of her.

I decided to run over to the big house, where I found Emily and Madam Charlotte. There they were, sitting in that beautiful front room of the house, the sitting room. It was hard to look at those two ladies growing old together without feeling the love they had pouring over into your heart. They were still very attractive women, despite their advanced years, but they no longer had the spark they'd once had. Losing Master Hoover and their sons had taken its toll.

They sat and reminisced, as old people like to do. They talked especially about how they missed and loved the same man for so many years. It was Master Hoover's birthday. Later that day Emily went into the room to feed Madam, but she was so weak that she couldn't eat. She never really got over losing Joel Edward, Percy, or her best friend, Master Hoover.

"Mother is tired, and I must ask you to please let me go, sweetheart," she had said to Emily in a soft voice. "You have been a perfect daughter." It seemed so difficult for her to talk. Emily could barely hear her voice, but she kept talking. "Mother is weary now. Please be happy for me, and let me go now." Emily put her arms around her. "Emily, I want to be at peace with my only love Percy and my best friend. They are waiting for me now. We will be waiting for you too, dear."

Emily held her like a baby, and she just kept on speaking her last words, "I have always loved you, Emily. You took good care of our boys." She reached for a large white envelope on the table. Her old fingers couldn't quite grasp it, so Emily helped her.

"Keep it," she said. "It's from both of us." The envelope was signed by Master Hoover and Mother Charlotte. When Emily opened the envelope, she saw papers.

"What are these?" she asked.

"Just look and you will see," Madam answered.

"But..." Emily's mouth dropped. The papers showed that she was married to Master Hoover. "When I was wearing your wedding dress..." she stopped, then continued. "The day Master Hoover died was meant to be my wedding day?" she asked.

Madam just looked at the joy on Emily's face and smiled.

Emily's eyes misted, remembering their honeymoon night by the river. Then she saw another document in the envelope, a will with the papers to the ranch. They had given the ranch to Emily and the children.

"Oh, Madam, he kept his promise to me," she said, and a smile came over her face.

Madam Charlotte was thrilled that she had lived to see that look on her daughter's face.

Emily looked into her mother's eyes and saw love, the very last expression they would share. She died with her eyes open, just like Master Hoover. Gently, Emily closed her eyes. As Emily held her in her arms, Madam Charlotte's heart just stopped.

Clarence Allen came into the room to check on them and found them, Emily was still holding her, rocking her in her arms and reminiscing about the first time she saw Madam Charlotte at the front door of the plantation. Emily seemed oblivious to her death, and kept speaking to her.

"I remember how you stood with Master Hoover the day he bought me from the slave auction," she was saying. "My mother, it seems like yesterday you was so young. Your beauty took my breath away."

Clarence gently took Emily's hand. She looked at him, grief-stricken.

"And now my mother is gone," she said, the finality of Madam Charlotte's death overcoming her. Emily cried as Clarence quietly took Madam Charlotte out of her arms.

I had tears in my eyes too. I couldn't picture Emily without Master Hoover, and especially without Madam Charlotte.

~

Well, the Hoovers' lives still moved ahead towards the future, bringing with them their memories of Master Hoover and Madam Charlotte. At family gatherings each year, they would tell the story of their family's struggle to survive. Emily had told them about her own family before she got to Hoover's Ranch. Though she had been taken from her mother, she had remembered and passed that knowledge on to her children.

Evan Lee, Emily's fifth son, married a very pretty slave girl named Elaine from Mr. Montgomery's place, a union arranged by Master Hoover before he died.

Master Hoover had set it up in such a way that they could pass for white, and many of them did for a time.

When people thought they were white, they didn't tell them any different, especially while Emily was alive. That was a way of protecting Emily.

CHAPTER 10

I was experimenting with closing my eyes to move ahead in time a little. I was trying to speed up time to the birth of my Big Daddy, but I wasn't having much luck.

Well, when I opened my eyes I didn't miss very much. It was just 1888. William Allen, my Big Daddy's father, had been born in 1866. There he was, already twenty-two years old, and handsome.

Wait! Oh my goodness! He is arguing with his father about something. I sat on the porch, watching them walk in the yard near the horses, but I couldn't hear their words. Their body language told me they were arguing, and I wanted to be able to hear them.

I ran out into the yard to get closer.

"You don't need to go gambling in town tonight," Clarence Allen Sr. told his son. "William, you are throwing away money," he said.

"Dad, I am twenty-two years old and you still treat me like I am twelve. I'll be back early. I am going to see my girl tonight, not to gamble."

His father was glad to hear him say that he was not going gambling; his son had been doing too much of that. So me, with my nosy self, I decided to follow William Allen

When he got into town there were beautiful people everywhere, all dressed up in style. It was a big to-do, some huge party, I'll say, but when I looked through the door where William was headed, it was a saloon.

Oh my goodness, he lied to his father, I thought. *That Hoover lying was in his blood. Here comes the deceit into another generation!*

This was not just any old party. It was high rollers gambling party. Wow! I don't remember Big Daddy telling me about this. William seemed to be the big man around town. Everyone was calling him Mr. Allen, and he liked it. He was hot in the gambling business, one of the best gamblers in that part of the country. He even had his own special table, and the ladies were all over him.

Those ladies had on the most elaborate dresses that I'd every seen, and I really wanted to be one of them just for a short time. So, I closed my eyes and made a wish. When I opened them, there I stood in an elegant blue dress. I looked across the room and I was watching myself standing there. *How can this be?* I wondered, watching myself.

As I looked across the room, my eyes stopped on William Allen. He was getting ready to play another hand of cards, but when he looked up his eyes found mine. We couldn't take our eyes off each other. He stood up at his table.

≈

"Deal me out," he said. He walked toward me and I felt my heart pounding.

Oh my goodness, he's good looking, I thought. *If I was going to be here looking for a man, why couldn't I spot someone else. He's my great grandfather, for God's sake. Why am I lusting after him?*

When he stepped in front of me I was speechless, and so was he for a second. We both talked at the same time,

"Hello."

Then we stopped again. He reached for my hand and I gave it to him. Kissing my hand he said,

"You are the most beautiful creature I have ever seen."

Well, I thought this was the best-looking man I'd ever seen too. But when he put his arms around me and asked me to dance, I looked around the room and noticed the other me watching.

"Where have you been all my life?" he asked. We smiled at each other, he held me close, and we danced far into the night.

Later we went outside the saloon, and walked through town. It was a beautiful night and the moon was full. I was excited when he asked me if I wanted to go for a ride in the moonlight.

"We could see the countryside together," he said.

"Yes, I would love to see the countryside with you," I answered.

We walked over to his carriage, and he lifted me inside. When I was in his arms, I felt like I was going

~

to melt. His light brown eyes were so sexy, and his lips so kissable. I wanted to hold him and kiss his beautiful lips.

The other me just stood over there in a daze. I couldn't believe what I was seeing. *They are going to leave me if I don't hurry*, I thought, so I started running. I accidentally ran right through the carriage and fell on the ground.

I was still wondering why there were two of me. *Maybe it's because of my wish*, I thought. The me on the ground noticed the carriage start to move with the other me sitting close to him. I ran after the carriage and when I caught up, I just jumped right into her lap. Oh my, I found myself inside of her.

"What's your name?" he finally asked.

"Tyara," I said, but he didn't hear me. The other me answered instead. "My name is Cora Smith," she said.

When she said her name, I realized that the woman wanting to make out with my grandfather wasn't me at all.

I was glad it was only my imagination too, but I do look a lot like her. I hadn't realized who she was. She would one day be my great-grandmother. When she revealed her name, it broke my spell. I found myself smiling. They were riding under the moonlight, but I didn't want to go with them because I didn't want to see my great-grandfather have sex with my great-grandmother, and possibly conceive my Big Daddy. So I jumped out of the carriage and

～

walked back to the saloon. Then I thought, *Now what am I supposed to do all alone, and at the saloon where there is gambling?* So, I thought I would find a place to sleep so I could speed up time. It worked, because as soon as I looked up I noticed that they were coming back in the carriage.

I ran near them so I could hear what they were saying. Unfortunately, I ran so fast that I went right through the carriage again and made it move this time. I even made the horses jump.

"The winds are really kicking up," he said.

I knew they would soon forget about the horses, and they did when they started kissing. On my part, I felt a strange sensation when I went through the horses, and I knew I was getting ready to go back to the future.

When I start feeling things like horses, it's time to go home, I thought to myself

I knew if I didn't pay attention to my feelings, I might remain in the past, and I would die.

They sat in the carriage looking into each other's eyes, and their minds drifted together. They were falling in love.

Cora said, "That was a nice ride under the moonlight, and by the way, William, are you always this romantic?"

"Are you always such a lady?" he answered, and I knew why they came back so quickly. They smiled at each other.

~

"I was trained to be a lady, and a good one," she said.

"Well, Cora, I am impressed with you. But there is something you need to know."

"Tell me," she said.

"I really want to see you again, but I don't know if you'll want to see me when you know who I am."

"It's funny that you said that because I was just thinking the same thing. Okay, you go first!"

"No! Ladies first," he countered.

"All right. I live on the Carson Plantation and I am a freed slave now. I look white because of my mother, but I am a mulatto and that means I am colored in the eyes of the law. But I could pass for white if I wanted too. " She was very surprised that he didn't get angry or even disappointed because she thought he was white. *If she only knew.*

Now he was more infatuated with her than ever. His family secrets weren't out in the open yet, so he didn't dare tell her he wasn't white either.

If I tell her now, he thought, *and she doesn't marry me, that could cause problems for the others*. He decided not to take a chance. The deceit continued.

She could tell that he had something that he was hiding, but he wasn't ready to share it. He was acting so understanding, and yet so quiet. Finally, he thought of something to say.

"I am the son of Clarence Allen. Do you know who he is?"

"Yes, I do," she said. "The Allen brothers are cousins to the Hoover's son, Edward Leon. I heard they were the richest men in these parts. I heard folks at my plantation talking about old man Hoover and Mr. Clarence Allen one day. Are you his son?"

"Yes, I am. When can I see you next?"

She was surprised that a white man in those parts would take a chance on going out with a mulatto girl. He waited patiently for her answer, but it was getting late and time for her to go home.

"Mr. Allen, it's not proper for a girl like me to be discovered dating a white man, if you know what I mean, sir." He was surprised by her answer, and then he realized that Master Hoover had protected them well.

"Madam Cora, you let me worry about that, unless you don't care to go out with me," he said. Then he took her into his arms and kissed her passionately. She didn't know what to think. Now I saw where my grandfather learned all of his romantic moves.

The Allen boys wanted to be proud of who they were. They respected their mother and that meant being proud of her heritage. For a while, they passed as white, as the Master had intended; but as each grew older, he made his own decision about who he wanted to be. Except for Edward Leon, who didn't know that he was colored, all of the Allen's eventually decided to live as colored men. Several of them joined groups which helped colored people.

I am glad I had this journey, because it helped me remember my childhood, and along with it the wonderful stories passed down to me by my grandfather and my mother. I realized how important it is to pass family heritage information down to each new generation.

I started to miss Mama Emily. I just couldn't get my mind off her. I felt like something bad was going to happen to her, and I had to find her. I knew I should be going back to my future, but instead I closed my eyes and made a wish to go back to the Hoover Ranch Plantation.

When I opened my eyes I was riding back with William to the big house. When I walked inside I saw Mama Emily. She looked terribly sad. I was so used to seeing her with Madam Charlotte, but here she was resting all alone, in her big chair in the sitting room. I walked over and sat in the chair where Madam Charlotte used to sit. Emily looked at me as though she could see me.

"Oh! Hello Madam," she said. "Oh my, how I've missed you." Mama Emily continued.

She seemed to see me, and thought I was Madam Charlotte.

"My goodness dear mother, you look young again, and I know you are waiting for me. Don't worry I'm almost ready to come to you," she said.

I didn't know what to say. I decided not to speak. What I did not want to do was disappoint her. It felt like old times to Emily, being with her Madam.

~

"Madam Charlotte, is that going to happen to me when I get there?" she asked. I didn't know what Emily was talking about so I just shrugged my shoulders.

"Oh, Madam Charlotte, you know what I am talking about. Will I get young again like you are now?"

I thought she couldn't see me, but I wasn't sure anymore, so I looked into her face. *Oh my goodness, I don't know what to do.* She was really talking to me, and the surprise showed on my face.

Emily stopped smiling, and said, "Why are you so sad, Madam? Please don't worry about me because I am coming with you real soon."

Then she closed her eyes and I thought she had died, so I ran into the other room to get Rosa's help, but was stopped by Mama Emily's voice.

"Madam Charlotte, don't leave me! I'm sorry. Sometimes I fall asleep in the middle of things."

I tried to comfort her by saying, "I remember Master Hoover falling asleep just like that." I forgot that I wasn't supposed to talk to her.

"Why are you calling him Master Hoover?" she asked, but didn't give me a chance to answer her. "That's right just before he died he would fall asleep," she answered. She was smiling again, and just as she was getting ready to talk, Rosa walked into the room, looking puzzled and glancing around.

"Rosa, did you lose something?" Emily asked. Rosa looked at her and smiled.

"Mama Emily, to what or to whom are you talking?"

"As a matter of fact, it's Madam Charlotte," said Emily.

"Madam?" This concerned Rosa. Perhaps Mama Emily was getting a bit senile in her old age. She pretended to clean up the area around the chair that I sat in. Rosa looked around the room for some kind of sign that would give Emily the idea that she was talking to the spirit of Madam Charlotte. She looked at the chair that Madam Charlotte used to sit in; I was in it, but she couldn't see me.

Emily laughed. I laughed too. I found myself staring at Rosa, realizing how much she reminded me of Miss Lilly, her mother. I found out through reading the papers and people talking that Miss Lilly had died about the time Dr. Pitts died, and I missed them both.

Emily was still laughing at me, and when I began to laugh she put up her hand to silence me. "No, Madam, Rosa will get mad, so try not to let her see you laughing."

"Mama Emily, now, trying to tell me that you see Madam Charlotte, that's one thing, but telling me that she is laughing with you is something else!"

I immediately became quiet.

"Well, I won't tell you a thing about Madam, daughter," said Emily. With that, she crossed her arms and looked away.

Clarence Allen, Sr., had come in and was smiling at his mother. "Mama Emily, is Rosa still harassing you?"

〜

"Yes, son! She loves to bother me, that wife of yours always gets after me!"

They all laughed, and so did I but this time Emily didn't tell me to stop. She loved Rosa a lot, even if Rosa did pick on her. They played with each other all the time.

"Where are the children?" Emily asked, then just dozed off to sleep while she was talking

"I'm worried about Mama Emily," said Rosa.

"Well she is nearly a hundred years old, honey."

"Clarence, I think she is ill. Maybe we should call a doctor. She falls off to sleep too often, and not only that, she was sitting here thinking she was talking to Madam Charlotte."

"Well, old folks will do that," said Clarence Allen.

They put Mama Emily to bed. She was now sleeping in the same room Madam Charlotte and Master Hoover had shared in the big house. When I walked into that room, I still expected to see Emily breast feeding one of the boys, laughing and talking with Madam Charlotte, just like the old days, but that wasn't the case this time. Emily slept so soundly when Clarence Allen and Rosa laid her down that they thought it was time to call everyone home.

Clarence sent a telegram to Edward Leon Hoover, Emily's seventh son, since he was out of state; he sent a telegram back, and telling him that he would get in touch with the others in Europe, California, New York, and Chicago. They all seemed to want the land after Emily died.

≈

They had planned to come home for the Christmas gala that Clarence Allen, Sr., sponsored each year, held downtown at the big saloon, but now it was only August.

Everyone headed home to see about Mama Emily.

One week later, everyone had arrived safely home from all over the country. Uncle Edward Leon Hoover and his wife Sheila Mae, their son Edward Earl, and his wife Carol Lynn all came from Washington, D.C. Aunt Eve, the widow of Madam Charlotte's only son, came from New York; her daughter Charlotte came with her. Uncle Joey Jon, his wife Jacqueline, and their two children David Roy, Jr., and Emily came from California. Willie Leroy's widow (he died in the Civil War), Aunt Betty Jane, brought their daughter Lilly, named after Miss Lilly; they came from Europe.

Clarence Allen, Sr., his wife Rosa; their son William Allen and his wife Cora; Evan Lee, his wife Elaine, their son Peter Joe; and me, Tyara from the future, we were all there on the ranch to honor our Mama Emily.

"She'll be with us for a week, if that long. She has pneumonia and is very weak." said Joey Jon, the doctor in the family.

The next day everyone settled in. The children played near the barn around the horses, and so did

I. We were outside playing, and I was having lots of fun even though only Mama Emily could see me.

I ran through the fields near the horses as if I were a child. Suddenly, a sensation came over me that stopped me in my tracks, a compelling force pulling me into the house. When I looked up, I found myself standing in Emily's room as she was trying to get out of bed. She had heard the children playing outside and wanted to look at them.

Oh my goodness, all of my life I've loved looking out the window at nature's grace. It always gave me peace, and so it does for Mama Emily, too, I thought.

I saw that she was about to fall, so I ran over and caught her. I was certainly surprised that I could touch her at all, but I was able to prevent her from falling.

"Oh my, thanks Madam."

I realized she still thought I was Madam Charlotte. She pointed toward the window and I understood that she wanted to look out the window some more, so I helped her to the window to enjoy the view.

"Madam Charlotte, I know you came for me, but you know that I must talk to the boys before we go," said Emily.

"Just take your time, I can wait," I found myself saying. "I'm not in no hurry." I don't know why I said it like that, the words felt strange to me.

Emily wanted to talk more, so I took her by the arm and helped her into bed. She laughed, and I forgot myself and began laughing too. I decided to talk to her like I was Madam Charlotte, just to make her feel better.

"What's so funny?" I said.

"I remember carrying you to bed by the arm when you were old and I was young," Emily said.

"Well it's my time to take care of you, because you were so good to me," I said affectionately.

Gazing into each other's eyes, I could see her loneliness for Master Hoover, and I could tell she wanted to ask me if I had seen him. Just as I was ready to tell her that I knew he was still in love with her, a cool wind came through the room and when it stopped, there he stood by the window.

He was as handsome as ever. He looked as young as he did the day that they met. Emily stared at him, hardly able to believe it was Master Hoover. She started to cry, reaching her arms toward him. He walked right past me and swept her into his arms, hugging her with intense passion.

"Sweetheart, I've come back for you, I have been waiting so long." Emily looked into his eyes.

"It's time," he said gently.

"Oh, my darling, I am ready. But first I must talk to our sons," said Emily.

The love in Master Hoover's heart shone through his eyes. Emily unexpectedly dropped off to sleep and Rosa came into the room. She seemed to sense something strange going on. She went to the window and looked out at the children, and I noticed that she was checking the window as though she thought it was open. When she found it closed she

~

walked back to the bed near where Master Hoover was sitting. He got up and stood nearby. Clarence Allen Sr. came in.

"Sweetheart, how is mother doing?" Rosa was still looking around the room as if she could feel us.

"Baby, does it feel cold in this room now?" Clarence Allen Sr. walked around the room and he almost walked right over Master Hoover.

"You know, sweetheart, it is a bit cold in here to me, but only in certain parts of the room, like next to mother's bed." Rosa looked at Emily. "Baby, why don't you stay here with your mother just for a moment, when she wakes up she may want to talk to you."

He pulled up a chair and sat down next to his mother's bed. I saw Master Hoover take a seat on the edge of the bed too, so I took a seat on the other side. In just a few moments, Emily opened her eyes.

"Oh sweetheart, you are still here." Clarence Allen thought she was talking to him. He began to wonder if Rosa was right about his mother. She seemed to be slipping away.

"Mother, who are you talking to? Are you talking to me?" he asked.

"Oh, you are still here too," said Emily. This time she was talking to me, thinking I was Madam Charlotte.

"Mother, are you talking to someone else in this room too?" her son asked.

She nodded. "Oh yes, son, don't you see my mother Charlotte and Edward?"

Her son no longer had any reason to doubt his wife. He started to tell her that Rosa was coming to give her a bath, but she stopped him. She knew she was running out of time.

"Send a telegram to the others and tell them to come home," she said.

"They are already home, don't you remember?" he asked.

"Oh yes." She smiled, and said, "Son, I am very tired, but I have something I need to say to all of my sons."

"Okay, Mother, I'll get them," he replied. Then he got his brothers, and everyone else came to pray with Mama Emily. The wives, cousins, and grandchildren knew: Mama Emily was slipping away. All of them had come immediately except Edward Leon, who made no effort to go with them. He was only there to hear the reading of the will, it was almost like he was waiting for her to die.

"Edward Leon, it is her wish to see you also," Clarence Allen said sternly. Edward Leon came along, and his son, Edward Earl, started following along with them.

"No. You stay with the kids, you can come in later," said Clarence Allen, Sr.

"Why is my father going if she asked for her sons only? He's not her son," Edward Earl wondered. He still didn't know that his father was Emily's son too.

When Emily woke up she looked right into Edward Leon's face.

He asked, "Mama Emily, are you cold?"

She answered, "No, my son."

"It seem cold in this room to me," he said.

Emily was just opening her eyes again, and smiling, of course. The boys thought she was smiling at them, so they smiled back. Edward Leon wondered why she called him her son.

"Come, lift up my pillow," she said, speaking to Edward Leon.

"That's right. Now I can see you all better."

Emily took a large envelope from under her sheets on her bed, handing it to Clarence Allen, Sr. "Read this, I've grown feeble and can't speak loud enough," she said.

He opened the document and began reading it to his brothers. It stated that they were Master Hoover's sons, inheriting the ranch together equally after the death of their mother Emily. The ranch was not to be sold, but passed down to the children. All members of the family would pay taxes on the property once a year. Any family member not sharing in the taxes would forfeit his or her part of the inheritance.

Edward Leon was not too happy about the inheritance being equal to the others, because he felt that Hoover Ranch should belong solely to him, since he was the only living Hoover.

"What! This is not right, this land belong to me only," he said.

When Emily heard his objection, she realized

that Edward had never told her son who he was, so she knew she must tell him before she passed.

"Listen to me, and you listen carefully. I am, and have been a Hoover for many years now. That's something I kept to myself," she said. Then she added, "I kept it to myself because it was done for me and for me alone."

Then Edward Leon said, "I knew all about that, Mama Emily, because father told me that you were my sister by a half-white colored woman." More lies.

"What else did he tell you, Edward Leon?" she asked.

"He told me that Madam Charlotte was not supposed to have any children because of her illness. So they took you from the slave women and raised you as a white girl. Now I find out that was just another one of my father's lies," he said sadly.

The spirit of Master Hoover, still sitting at the edge of Emily's bed, knew he shouldn't have left this task for Emily to do or undo. Emily reached under her sheets again and pulled out another document.

"Read it. Read it for yourself and for all your brothers." It was a marriage certificate. When Edward Leon saw what it was, he was outraged.

"This can't be true, it's dated the day my father died," he yelled.

Even the other sons didn't know about this, and they all were surprised. Emily said, "Edward Leon, it was the day he died, but that was my wedding day also, and you were there and so were your broth-

230 · *Millie L. McGhee*

ers," she informed him. She went on to say, "Master Edward Hoover and Madam Charlotte wanted to surprise me that day. But my sweetheart was too weak, and he had to be taken back to bed. Before he died, though, he married me." Then she looked at her son and said, "Don't you remember, Edward? Just before your father's death, he signed the certificate because he wanted me to become his wife. He had never been married before. I was a Hoover then, and I am one now. Before he died he gave the marriage certificate to Sister Harriet to give to Madam, and Madam Charlotte could have burned it, but she didn't. Madam Charlotte knew we loved each other, and she was happy for me." She paused for a moment, "Later I told Madam Charlotte to keep it because if I filed it, I thought it would cause trouble for all of us. I kept it a secret, but Madam Charlotte filed it for me anyway."

I am sure Emily didn't think things were going to happen this way. If she had only known that Master Hoover had never told Edward Leon the truth, she would have handled this differently. At that moment, the pastor came in to pray for Mama Emily.

"Is there anything I can do?" he asked, noticing the tension.

"No, thank you. It's a family affair, I'll handle it, you should wait in the other room, this is private," Edward Leon told the pastor.

"You might want to respect a man of the cloth,"

admonished Emily gently. "God don't like ugly. You know I taught you to respect the Lord."

Her seventh son looked embarrassed. "I didn't mean to be disrespectful," he muttered.

"Any of the rest of you have any disagreements, with my marriage or anything else?" she asked.

Emily had to take a deep breath to say that, but it was important to clear the air. No one had a problem except Edward Leon, and Joey Jon had a problem with how Edward Leon was acting. Mama Emily had told him that Edward Leon was his real brother, and he didn't mind. He wondered why Edward Leon couldn't accept it.

"If you are a Hoover, doesn't that change all our names to Hoover?" Joey Jon asked.

"Maybe years ago it could have been done with no trouble to anyone, but it isn't feasible to change all the names now," she said.

"That is not true! You all have to go under the name of your own father, and he is Harry Carson," Edward Leon said.

Emily never liked Harry after she found out about Sweet Anna, so this didn't make her too happy. "Harry was never the father of any of my babies, you remember that, my son," she said to Edward Leon.

By this time Joey Jon had heard just about enough from Edward Leon and said, "Listen here, Edward Leon, I've had enough of your attitude. You have the same father and mother we have. So sit your butt down and shut up, because I'm sick of you and your high and mighty attitude."

Clarence Allen stood up and sternly said, "Now Joey Jon, that is not right. Edward doesn't know all what we know, and we are all forgetting that we owe Mama Emily respect." He paused. "Just remember that Mama Emily is ill, and we may be losing her. Tell me, is this what we want to send her away with, a lot of hatred between her sons?"

I took one look at Master Hoover's spirit. He was proud of Clarence Allen, just like when he was alive. I noticed that all of the boys respected Clarence. They all got very quiet.

Joey Jon stood up. "I'm sorry Edward Leon," he said and then went to the bed and sweetly kissed his mother.

"You boys are the kind of sons I'm proud of," she said. Then she said, "Thank you, Clarence and Joey Jon."

"Mama Emily, maybe we should all leave the room and let you talk to Edward Leon alone. I'm sure he needs to speak to you privately," said Clarence Allen.

I could see that Master Hoover agreed with Clarence Allen.

"Okay. You all come back and see me when we're finished," she said.

Each of the boys kissed her, including Edward Leon. After they had all left the room except Edward Leon, he went to Mama Emily and laid his head on

~

her chest. He began to sob. Edward Leon had lived all of his life believing a lie. Emily placed her arms around his head and talked softly to him.

"Edward Leon, I am sorry to be the one to give you pain, but I must tell you the truth. Maybe you will pass it on to your children and stop the pain, and maybe you won't, but it is time for truth. That is your choice. Just remember if you don't tell them the truth you will be doing the same thing to your children that your father did to you."

She looked into his eyes. Even at her age, her eyes shone with a gentle light.

"Now, I want you to listen to me. First of all, I am your natural mother, which means you came from my body. Master Hoover is your father, he is the only man that I have ever had from the age of twenty, and he is the father of all seven of my sons. You were my seventh son, and he picked you out over all the others because he wanted you to carry his name into the future, so you had to be raised as a white child. He loved all of his sons, but I think he loved you more, and you should be proud."

"Why did he love me more?" asked Edward Leon.

"Your father felt that you were the best gift that he could have given to Madam because he couldn't give her his love, so he gave her our love, and that was you." Edward Leon was surprised at that answer. Emily went on to say, "You didn't look any better than the others, nor did you look any whiter than they did, but you were born on a very special day—Madam Charlotte's birthday.

"Now, when I told your brothers he didn't give them his last name, they were angry and very disappointed with him too, but most of all they felt like they must have been different. Despite that, I taught them to be proud of the fact that they were getting a chance in life," She paused. "I told them that lots of slaves were beaten and hungry, but we were not, and it was because of Master Hoover you don't know what it was like to be a slave."

Emily rarely talked about it, but she told Edward Leon how hard it was for her, growing up as a slave before Master Hoover bought her.

"I was born a slave, but when Master Hoover brought me home from that slave auction and took me to the arms of Madam Charlotte; my new mother, it was then and only then, that my life was worth living."

The spirit of Master Hoover looked as though he was weeping, sitting there at the end of the bed. Edward Leon raised his head and looked into his mother's face, with his eyes full of tears.

"Did Madam Charlotte love you too?"

"Yes, son, she did. She took me in her arms, protected me, and raised me like I was her own child. She protected me from all men and she taught me everything I knew, but most of all she taught me how to love. When I turned twenty years old she turned me over to Master Hoover because she knew he was in love with me from the beginning."

Her son was starting to feel better about things, and he began to understand what it was like being born a slave.

"You know, Edward Leon, I wanted to have even more babies after you were born," she confessed.

"Why didn't you?" he asked.

"Well, Master Hoover just got too old, or maybe God just felt seven was enough. All my boys were conceived in love and passion. We both knew that our love was forever, and I know he still loves me even now." Emily looked at his spirit sitting there on the edge of the bed smiling at her, waiting to take her away with him forever.

I could see that she was getting weaker and weaker.

"Son, don't hate your father and me. You boys were our joy, and when he asked me to let you carry his last name and wanted you to be raised as a white child, it made me proud. Edward Leon, the memory you had of your father before today was good, so keep it, because he was a good man. He asked God for forgiveness on his deathbed for all of his wrong-doing, any pain and hurt that he may have caused anyone, and God has forgiven him. And now, son, I am asking you to forgive us both."

"There is nothing to forgive. You were always a good mother, even though I was told you were my sister. I just want to know one more thing," he said. "What did Madam Charlotte do all of those years without a man, during the time her husband was sleeping with a slave girl and having seven children with her?" he asked.

"Their marriage was what you call a forced marriage. Madam Charlotte was in love with another man."

"Yes, but she didn't go off and sleep with him."

"Son, whatever Madam Charlotte did, it is not up to us to judge. I know that she asked God for forgiveness for her sins also, before she died. It is true that Joel Edward might have been her lover's son. Now, I am telling you to stop the secrets that have caused so much pain in all of our lives. I am trying not to keep secrets from you anymore." said Emily. She went on to say, "So you see, son, things are not always what they seem." Emily closed her eyes again, but this time she didn't open them anymore. The door opened and it was all of the boys and their wives.

I looked in the corner of the room by the window, and was surprised to see the spirits of Emily's three dead sons, standing there, waiting for her too.

"Hello boys, you came for me too?" Emily spoke softly, but only the spirits and I could hear her. Master Hoover stood waiting, with his arms folded. It was very romantic, the way he sat there waiting for her soul to leave her body and come with him. A glow came over Emily, her spirit became younger, and she looked like she did the day of her coming out party.

I looked at Master Hoover as he stood up like he was getting ready to leave. He and Emily took each other's hands and started toward the window, along with their three sons, and also Madam Charlotte leaving my body. I followed them through the window, and noticed others: Miss Lilly, Willie, Harry, Sweet Anna, Percy Carson, Dr. Pitts, and many others. It looked like they were all there to celebrate Mama Emily's home going.

"She is gone now," the doctor was saying, and he covered her face.

I watched until I couldn't see them any longer. They vanished into a beautiful white flash into the clouds.

Edward Leon had come to terms with the news, but he wasn't sure of what to do next. He looked in the eyes of his brothers and started talking. "I am in a spot with my wife and her parents, they won't understand if I tell them I'm a colored man. They are prejudiced against colored people and so am I. All this time they thought I was white, and so did I. What do you think I should do?" he asked his brothers.

"Just leave it be for now, don't tell anyone anything different," they advised

I could see the relief on his face. A heavy burden was lifted from Edward Leon when he made the decision to pass for white forever. He loved his wife and her father, and they thought the world of Edward. Why should his world crumble just because of a drop of blood from another race was running through his veins?

The deceit goes on.

≈

CHAPTER 11

I turned to go back into the house, but I felt very tired and sleepy. I noticed it was late. There sat the carriage, so I climbed into the back just to take a nap and immediately fell into a deep sleep. But apparently only for seconds, because I soon heard laughter and music and opened my eyes.

I realized that I was still in back of the carriage, so I sat up and looked out, and found that I was alone in front of the saloon. Everything looked different, and then I realized it was the Christmas decorations. I could hear the most beautiful sounds of Christmas, a group of colored people caroling. Everyone was beautifully dressed in holiday colors, and joyously singing. I heard an amazing voice.

I know that voice, that beautiful voice, I thought.

I looked out of the carriage and it was Sister Harriet. I loved to hear her sing, so I just sat for awhile and enjoyed the music. Around her stood a group of children who sang like nothing I'd ever heard or seen in my world.

I must have nearly drifted off to sleep again, because time sped up and the next time I looked I saw a sign in front of the saloon: The 1895 HOOVER & ALLEN Holiday Gala.

The festive streets were filled with people dressed in holiday fashions. I wanted to look pretty too, so I closed my eyes and made a wish. When I opened my eyes, I was dressed up, and I looked stunning, if I do say so myself.

The dress that I was wearing was velvet, and my favorite color green. I even wore makeup, and my hair was in an up-do. It made me feel like a queen. I started to climb out of the carriage and just as I put one foot on the ground, I felt a hand. I was shocked that someone could see me, touch me, and I could feel it. How strange.

I heard a voice speaking to me, and I was afraid. How could they see me? When I got both feet on the ground, I turned to see who had my arm. He was a good-looking, half-white gentleman. I could tell he was colored by his beautiful lips and nice curly hair.

"Are you lost?" he said gently.

I didn't know what to do or say. I stood speechless, but I knew that he could tell I was lost.

"You must be looking for the Hoover and Allen gala. It's at the Mid Town Saloon."

I didn't know how to respond so I walked a little further trying to regain my composure. I couldn't help but turn to him again, though. "Yes, I am, sir! I am lost!"

"Where do you come from?" he asked.

∼

240 · *Millie L. McGhee*

I could tell he was very intelligent and he was charmingly polite. *He must be an Allen*, I thought.

"I live across the river, sir," I said, deciding I'd have to make it up as I go.

"May I escort you to the door?" he asked. Something about him made me feel elegant. Like royalty, I extended my hand, yet I wondered who he was.

"Sir, and what might be your name?"

He looked at me for a moment, a smile playing at the edges of his lips. "My name is Peter Joe Allen, madam. And who are you?"

I didn't know what to do then, so I came up with another name. How could I tell him I was an Allen too? He'd wonder why he didn't know me, if I was family.

"My name is Ruby Dee, sir."

This seemed to satisfy him. Arm in arm, we walked to the Mid Town Saloon where a party was going strong. He opened the door for me. I held Peter Joe's arm as he ushered me in. The saloon was adorned with festive holiday decorations. Dinner tables were arranged around the room.

I was almost giddy as the spirit of the holiday surrounded me, with everyone laughing, dancing, and having a good time. And everyone, I realized, was my own relative. *I really am a part of the past*, I thought, and began to relax.

Peter put his lips close to my ear and said, "Uncle Clarence Allen, Sr., rented the saloon for the family party." Then he said, "He is my great-great Uncle! The Hoovers started this Christmas celebration many years past. Since Master Hoover and Joel Edward Hoover have passed away, Clarence Allen, Sr., continues the tradition."

I looked around the room and saw William Allen and his wife Cora carrying a new baby. This baby was my Big Daddy, Clarence Allen, named after Uncle William's father in his mother's arms! I knew he would grow to be almost seven feet tall, but here he was tiny.

It would be hard to describe to anyone how wonderful it felt to actually be part of this celebration with my ancestors. It made me feel so very special. I was happy, but then I realized a terrible truth.

It must be 1895, I thought. *That's around the time my Big Daddy was a child.* I was the only one at the party from the future that knew about a terrible truth that was going to happen to the family in the year 1895.

When I looked at Big Daddy's mother across the room I remembered that night when she went with him on the moonlight ride. I then realized how much I looked like her. My great-grandparents stood there: Cora Smith Allen, holding her newborn baby, and her handsome husband, William Allen, there with his arms around her body. I looked around the room to see who else was still alive and who was attending this event. I was excited and I knew that I needed to relax because I wanted to enjoy myself and everyone could see me now, or so I thought.

No one really paid any attention to Peter Joe and I, standing there at the door, except for one cousin's hello and smile toward Peter Joe. As the party went on, I let go of his arm while one of his cousins, who he called Charlotte, began speaking to him. She must be the daughter of Madam Charlotte's son Joel Edward, I thought. He'd been killed in the war. Charlotte took Peter Joe by the arm just as though I wasn't with him.

"Come on, Peter Joe, let's go see the others."

I was left standing there alone. She sure didn't notice me, and I think Peter Joe forgot about me as he wandered off with her. Charlotte was very pretty and just as kind as her grandmother, Madam Charlotte.

I felt lonely, so I decided to mingle. I set out to find out who was attending this party. I saw our host, Clarence Allen, Sr., and his wife, my great-great-grandmother Rosa Allen. They were sitting together in a lounging chair, talking. She looked to be about eighty-one years old, but Rosa was still so pretty, and they were holding hands. *It seems that the Allen boys are very romantic*, I thought.

Well, maybe the women who married Allen men were pretty, but if I must say so myself, the Allen boys were the best looking men I'd had seen so far.

I saw Uncle Edward Earl Hoover and his prejudiced wife from Washington D.C, whom no one liked, Aunt Carol Lynn. They brought their five-year-old son who they called "J.E." to the gala. They only came to see if the Allen boys would keep there secret, and to tell them that this was their last time coming to this Christmas party

～

Uncle Edward Earl's father, Edward Leon Hoover, was also in attendance with his wife, Aunt Sheila Mae Hoover. Edward Leon worked in the Pentagon in Washington D.C., just like his son.

My favorite cousin here, already, was certainly Peter Joe. His parents, Uncle Evan Lee Allen and his wife Aunt Elaine, were both at the party. I noticed Aunt Eve Hoover Piece. She was the wife of Joel Edward Hoover, Master Hoover's only son with Madam Charlotte Hoover. Well, that's what everyone thought, but since I'd been there I knew he could have been the son of her lover Percy Carson. That secret went to the grave with them.

After the death of Joel Edward, Aunt Eva remarried. Her daughter, named after Madam Charlotte, was attending the gala with her mother and stepfather, Mr. Fred Piece. They moved around a lot because of his job. At this time they were living in New York, but they kept in touch with the family often and weren't about to miss the party.

Despite secrets and deceit, the Hoover and Allen families remained close for many years. And my New York relatives weren't the ones that traveled the greatest distance to attend: Aunt Betty Jane brought Little Lilly home for Christmas, all the way from Europe. Betty Jane had been married to Uncle Willie Leroy, who met her when he was in the Army. He was one of Emily's seven sons, and had named his little daughter after Miss Lilly just before his death.

Well, the name was about all Little Lilly had in

common with Miss Lilly. Her character left a lot to be desired. She was very pushy and bossy and loved to start trouble.

Little Lilly was nothing like Miss Lilly, whose cooking and housekeeping cared for the Hoover family for so many years. Miss Lilly had passed away, but everyone had called her their "Big Mama" at one time or another. Everyone loved Miss Lilly, and during the end of her life they took especially good care of her.

It was said that when Miss Lilly lost Willie, it seemed as though she gave up. I will always remember her talks with Emily. When she talked about Willie, she'd say, "I loved that man."

I really missed seeing Master Hoover, Madam Charlotte, Emily, Miss Lilly, Harry, Willie, Sweet Anna, old Master Montgomery (Madam Charlotte's brother) and Dr. Pitts. All were dead now. It was sad.

Also attending the party—all the way from California—were Uncle Joey Jon Allen and his lovely wife, Aunt Jacqueline Allen. I felt proud that he was Dr. Joey Jon Allen, the first doctor in the family. They brought their two children with them: David Roy, named after his brother (who died in the Civil War), and Emily, named for Mama Emily.

It was difficult getting used to the new generation. I missed seeing the excitement of Emily and Master Hoover's electrifying romantic encounters. Loving each other deeply, they carried secrets and deceit to the grave.

~

My ancestors socialized together in groups; all the young people stuck together, laughing and having fun. Wanting to have some fun too, I decided to walk over to see what was making my cousins laugh. I felt like I knew them already. I also wanted to see if I could recognize cousins, aunts, and uncles that I'd meet living in the future.

"Peter Joe!" I called out to him, but I don't think he heard me.

So, I walked closer. They were laughing at Peter Joe for some reason, and he looked sad.

"Peter Joe, I think you really need to tell your parents about your hallucinations." Lilly said, with her characteristic lack of tact.

Charlotte stepped up. "Hush, Lilly Allen, you don't know what you are talking about. Come on, Peter Joe."

She took Peter Joe by the arm and started walking away with him. That made Lilly angry. "You hush yourself, Charlotte Hoover, you're just taking his side because you have a love-thing for him."

The blushing Charlotte stopped walking and looked at Lilly angrily. She was embarrassed and Peter Joe was rather surprised at what Lilly said. Charlotte walked right up and stood in Lilly's face. Charlotte could no longer hold her tongue.

"Peter Joe is my cousin and you don't deserve to be named after Miss Lilly, because you are nothing like her. She was a much better person than you, and you'll never be like her!"

≈

246 · *Millie L. McGhee*

Wow! I looked over to see what was going on with their parents. The mothers were coming our way. When Charlotte finished talking to Lilly everyone looked shocked, and so did I.

Aunt Jacqueline spoke first. "Don't talk to each other like that!"

It wasn't just a fight they were concerned about. With the thoughtless way the children were talking, they worried that someone might slip and blurt out a family secret right in front of the guests.

"Don't gossip about what goes on in the family," she admonished.

The mothers hovered around, but the fathers went back to their corners and continued their drinking, laughing, and telling jokes about their sex lives. It was understood that it was the mother's job to keep the children in line.

For instance, I listened to Aunt Carol Lynn talking to her five-year-old son, J.E. Hoover. I don't think I'll ever forget that conversation. She took him into a corner and said quietly, "J.E., you listen to me, don't get involved in any of that 'nigger' talk. We are here only out of respect to your white side of the family. You and Charlotte are the only children here that are pure white, no nigger blood in you."

"But they are my cousins. They aren't niggers," said Little J.E. .

"You'll understand better when you're older," she said.

"They look white like me," said J.E., looking confused.

~

"When we go back to Washington, we'll have a talk about what a nigger is. This is not the time," said Aunt Carol Lynn.

Aunt Carol had no idea that she was married to a man with colored blood, and her husband Edward Earl didn't even know the secret himself because his father had never told him. The lie he lived was passed down to his only son Edward Earl Hoover, who was now going to be passing it down to his only son J.E. Hoover.

It was a hard decision, but Edward Leon planned to tell everyone at the family's gala. He was getting up in age and he felt it was time for them to know.

I looked across the room, and noticed Uncle Edward Leon all alone. He had walked away from his brothers, and was standing in front of a window in deep thought. I walked over to him hoping that I would be able to speak to him, wanting to see if he'd notice me, and maybe I could make him feel better. I felt sad for him. Just as I got ready to speak to him, his brother Joey Jon walked up.

"Hey, brother Edward, what's going on with you? Is everything all right?"

Edward Leon looked at his brother with eyes full of pain. "I'm in turmoil inside, and I don't know how much longer I can keep living this lie," he said.

They took a seat at one of the tables to talk.

Clarence Allen, Sr., who was now growing old in age, was talking to his brother Evan Lee, who was also up in age. Edward Leon looked older than both of them, even though he was younger. It was said that he looked older because of the stress of hiding the truth for so many years.

Edward Leon felt that he couldn't tell the truth about his bloodline, because he thought he would lose everything he loved, and everything he worked for all those years. In the capitol of the United States, you didn't get good government positions if you were of mixed blood.

Clarence Allen, Sr., and Evan Lee finally joined Edward Leon and Joey Jon. All of the brothers were good friends just like Emily had prayed they would be, and they remained that way until they all died.

The brothers were ready to help free Edward Leon's mind of his fears. Brother Evan Lee stated, "You don't need to worry about family secrets, because it's all safe. Master Hoover already protected us, and our secrets, in every way possible."

They reassured him.

"Brother Edward Leon, your life is safe with us, our father was 'The Master of Deceit' and we know how to keep a secret. We love you, and we'll protect you forever. Your secret is safe with us, go on living just as you have. You are a white man, and that is the way it's going to stay," said Clarence Allen, Sr.

All of the brothers came to a decision to meet with all of their sons and tell them the truth. They would tell only their sons because they were sure that the men of the family would honor the family secret.

We were having fun at the party. I was reminisc-

~

ing a lot about family history, and I was learning a lot more about my heritage and ethnicity so that when I went home it would be a good story to tell.

It was still 1895, and now I find myself going in all different directions wanting to get to know more about the Washington, D.C., Hoovers. I was still at the gala, and wanted to know more, it was hard to settle down and take it as it came, so I found a way to stop thinking ahead and take one moment at a time.

Well, when I collected my thoughts, I went back to the party. I started mingling again, looked across the room, and spotted Peter Joe. I wondered why he was sitting there looking so unhappy. I decided to go over and cheer him up. I had taken a liking to him because he looked so much like my brother Vincent. Now I had an idea of what Vincent was going to look like when he grew up.

I walked over and sat down next to Peter Joe.

"Hello beautiful, where have you been?" he asked.

Just as I sat down with him, and cousin Charlotte walked up. "Peter Joe, why are you sitting here talking to yourself?"

I realized that for some reason, he was able to see me, but no one else could. All evening, we had thought everyone could see me. I thought they were not talking to me because I was a stranger.

Peter Joe looked at me and he remembered how I had just appeared, hanging on to the carriage. One minute I wasn't there, and the next minute I was right in front of him. "You know, you just popped in front of me like a ghost. Are you a figment of my imagination?" he asked. Peter Joe was really looking worried. "Maybe I am loony," he said.

I felt so sad, and trying to cheer him up made things worse. I wanted to do something to make it up to him, but didn't know what. I looked up, and all the kids were running towards us.

Little Lilly spoke up. "I was right, Charlotte! Now you should stop taking up for him and stay away from that loony." Laughing, they all walked away, dragging Charlotte by the hand.

Peter Joe really felt bad then, he got up and ran out on the terrace of the saloon. He was hurt and sad. I followed him out. "Get away from me, I'm bad news, can't you see? I'm loony."

"No, you are not a loony, you are brighter than any one of them," I said.

"I wish that were true, then they would have to apologize to me for all the times that they hurt me."

"Peter Joe, my name is not Ruby Dee; I am your cousin from the future, and I was born in 1947. In your time, I would not have been born yet!"

Peter Joe stared at me, and said, "You know, I believe you. But they are never going to believe that."

"No, they won't believe it, and you are not going to tell them about me," I said.

"Well, how am I ever going to get them to like me?" he asked.

"We'll think of something to do together," I said.

Despite the problems, Peter Joe was excited about

~

meeting me. He wanted to know if I knew what his life was going to be like, and how long he was going to live. I told him that I did, but I was not going to tell him. "Telling you would be bad luck. No one should try to change the future or alter any part of the past," I said.

"We should just try to make our futures better by trying to make a difference," he said.

I was so proud of him. Then I knew why he was able to see me, and no one else could. It was because he was special.

"Okay, I will tell you a little about your future," I said. He got excited.

"Tell me, please?" he asked.

"You will live a long good-life, many people will like you, and though you don't realize it right now, but you are chosen by God."

Feeling better, we started thinking of a way to change his cousins' minds about him. All at once he turned and looked at me. He had an idea, and I had one too.

"Okay, you go first!" I said.

"If you could fly, I could tell them that I have magic powers," he said.

"Well, I can't fly and I don't think that's a good idea, because I'm not sure what I could do if I could fly," I said.

"Well, what is your idea?" he asked.

"I'm trying to think of something to make your cousins believe in you." I could see that made him happy.

$\backsim$

"Well how can you do that?" he asked.

"I know something no one else knows. It will happen in your future, and it may not be good. But you can tell it to them before it happens, and when it does happen they'll think you have great powers, and that you can predict the future," I said.

Peter Joe thought that was a great idea.

"Now," I began. "They are not going to believe you until it happens, but don't worry about that. When it really happens they will respect you forever."

He got so excited he hugged me. He seemed surprised that he could feel me, and no one else could see or hear me. He was very impatient and was holding me tight.

"Let go, so I can think of something to tell you." I thought for a moment, then said, "This is the only thing I can think of but it is not good news. As a matter of fact it's downright awful, and very sad."

"Oh my! What?" He was excited, but after thinking about it, I didn't want to tell him. "Please, I've got to know. Please, tell me, even if it's awful. It's got to be something big, to get their attention."

I hope Peter Joe doesn't think he can change this or try to stop it from happening, I was thinking. "Nothing I tell you can ever be changed, altered, or stopped because it has already happened in the future," I explained.

That didn't change his mind. "What is the awful tragedy that is going to strike and change many lives?" he asked, starting to get impatient.

∽

"Okay! Remember, I didn't want to tell you. In 1895, Uncle William Allen will be killed by outlaws in town, but I don't know when or where."

He stared at me. "Oh! My God! This is 1895."

I felt terrible. How could I be so insensitive? I totally forgot that William Allen was his favorite uncle. Peter Joe was heartbroken. He started crying and ran into the other room repeating, "That's not true, that can't be true."

When he entered the party in tears, shouting those words, the party stopped. His uncle William Allen had left a short time ago with two men, who had come into the saloon telling him about a man in town who was looking for him, angry about the last card game that they'd played together. The man had lost his life savings to Uncle William Allen and said he felt cheated. He was accusing Uncle William Allen of stacking the deck. Uncle Evan Lee heard Peter Joe crying. He and Aunt Elaine ran over to their son.

"What's wrong, son?" he asked.

The whole family had fear in their eyes. It wasn't like Peter Joe to become emotional like this.

"Father, Uncle William Allen will be killed tonight," his father held him close after he looked into his eyes.

He could tell that his son was frightened and that it was real. I was so sorry that I told him. I knew now it was the wrong thing to do. The whole family thought that Peter Joe must be ill, and they were all very concerned about him.

～

"Who told you that awful lie? Was it Little Lilly?" his father asked. Peter Joe stopped them from going after Lilly.

"No. It's just something I know, from inside of my heart."

His father, Evan Lee and mother Elaine were getting ready to take him home when they heard a loud sound outside in the streets. Alarmed, all the men got together and went to see if anything had happened. While they were gathering to go out, Clarence Allen, Sr., noticed that his son wasn't back in the saloon.

"He went down the street with a couple of friends earlier, but he hasn't returned," said Joel Jon.

Peter Joe and the other young adults had to stay inside the saloon with the ladies, while the men went to check out the loud noise down the street.

I felt so bad. I walked over to Peter Joe and he grabbed my hand.

"I'm going to go and see what happened, since no one can see me," I said.

Holding my hand, Peter Joe said, "No, don't leave me."

"I'll be right back with some information," I told him in a soft voice.

He was holding my hand so tight. "Please don't leave me," he begged.

His mother was sitting with him and thought he was talking to her. "I am not going to leave you Peter Joe," she answered.

∼

Then I said, "Peter Joe, I am not leaving you, I will always be with you." He finally let go of my hand.

I ran out the door passing the men so I could get there first. Oh my goodness! It was William Allen but it was too late. He was already dead. I watched the men trying to help him, but they couldn't bring him back. I turned and ran back to the saloon to tell Peter Joe.

When I got back all the music was off, everyone was sitting with Peter Joe and Aunt Cora, who was suddenly a widow, although she didn't know it. She was holding her three-week-old son who would become my Big Daddy (Clarence Allen, Jr.) someday. He had just lost his father, who was only twenty-nine years old, and he would never get a chance to know him.

Little Lilly and Charlotte and all the other cousins and friends had walked over to Peter Joe when I returned. He looked into my eyes and got up right away, moving closer to Aunt Cora and the baby. He put his arms around her and sat down. No one spoke, but I spoke to Peter Joe in a very soft voice,

"Uncle William Allen is dead on the ground in a puddle of blood, shot in the head and stomach." Of all the memories coming back to me, this was one I'd wished that I didn't have.

Everyone noticed Peter Joe as he looked up toward the door where I was standing, only they couldn't see my tears. "He can't be dead—shot in the head and stomach—who shot him?" Peter Joe was beside himself with grief.

≈

Aunt Cora looked at Peter Joe. "Who's shot in the head and stomach, Peter Joe?" she said.

All the kids stared at Peter Joe with respect; they no longer believed he was loony. Meanwhile the men found William Allen down the street, alone, lying face down dead, with blood running out the sides of his mouth. His father, Clarence Allen, Sr., was kneeling, devastated. He picked up his dead son's head, put it in his lap, and cried like a baby as he held him.

The men helped carry the body to a carriage brought over to take the body to the coroner's office. They walked back to the saloon with his father.

"Why my son, why not me?" said Clarence Allen, Sr., quietly.

When they walked through the door, his wife Rosa was already crying, unable to comprehend that her son was dead. So was everyone else. As the men came in, they wondered if something else had happened, because no one had come back to tell them about the shooting.

"What happened?" Evan Lee asked.

"Peter Joe told us that Uncle William was shot in the head and is dead on the ground," said Lilly.

"And how did Peter Joe find out?"

Peter Joe said, as he stood up, "I got a feeling in my heart, and a spirit told me."

Only two weeks before Christmas, the tragedy caused such pain to the family. The celebration was over.

~

"A death before Christmas, that's pretty sad," said little cousin Charlotte. That was exactly what I was thinking.

Soon we were all on our way back to Hoover Ranch with Aunt Cora, trying to comfort her. I found myself crying, because that baby was my Big Daddy. I got into the carriage with Peter Joe and rode with them. When we arrived at the ranch, little Charlotte and Lilly wanted to help take care of the baby, and so did I, but nobody could see me except Peter Joe.

Aunt Cora was so upset. "My son will never know his father," she said, starting to cry. Peter Joe hugged her. All family members stayed with her and the baby until she was exhausted and fell asleep.

This Christmas celebration, which began in such special delight for me, had ended in deep sadness. Complete silence reigned throughout the house.

When we arrived I noticed that the ranch looked different to me. It had been rebuilt with real lights and a new fence around it. When we arrived inside the house, I couldn't understand my feelings. I felt so sad that I decided that it was time for me to go back home, so, I got up to leave. Peter Joe must have seen me leaving and ran after me.

I turned and started walking away, but the next thing that I knew, he had me by the arm. He wanted to talk to me.

"Thanks, Ruby Dee, and please don't be sad because you told me what was going to happen. It's not your fault and it did help me. You see, everyone looks up to me and believes in me now, just as you told me it would be," he said.

I was happy about that, but in my spirit I knew I had to go now. Then I heard Peter Joe's father, Uncle Evan Lee, talking to Uncle Edward Leon from Washington, DC. They were ready to leave and go home. I wondered why they wanted to leave so soon; this made me want to follow them to learn more about them after the Christmas Gala.

I felt sleepy, and I knew it was time to go. I started to fade in and out of Peter Joe's sight. I heard him calling for me, and I opened my eyes for a moment.

"Please don't leave me, you promised me you'd never leave me!" Peter Joe said.

"Peter Joe, I told you that I'll always be with you in spirit, and I will, but I need to leave now or I will die in the future. We can't change the future." I now wanted to live more than ever, and I had a strong reason for it. "I need to tell my family the story about all of you. I love you, Peter Joe," I said hurriedly. Then everything vanished.

When I opened my eyes, I was in Uncle Edward Leon's home in Washington, DC. Time must have move forward in their time zone, because they were home. I decided to put off going home, back to my time, for a while and see what I could learn about this side of the Hoover and Allen family in Washington, DC.

I moved through time so fast, and couldn't stop it, but I don't think I wanted to anyway. While back in time in Washington, DC, I remembered look-

~

ing at a handwritten book in the family library. It stated that three of Master Hoover's sons were registered in records in the town hall in Mississippi. The book also said that the Allen's were relatives of the Hoovers. This was a book that was given to Edward Leon by his brothers to keep in case he needed to tell his family the truth someday. Later, I would find out what the records would show in my own time era, but here the Allen boys were listed like this:

Clarence Allen, Sr.

Son of Emily Allen, a white woman born 1793. A relative of Master Edward D. Hoover

That was the way Master Hoover protected them all. All of Emily's sons were listed this way. All of the sons born by Emily were named Allen, except one. Edward Leon was registered in the town hall of records with the name Hoover. Master Hoover's son by his white wife, Joel Edward, who died in the Civil War, was listed also as a Hoover.

After the big 1895 holiday gala, lots of changes were made with regard to the future of Hoover Ranch. When Edward Leon Hoover returned to Washington, he realized that his life was in good hands with his Mississippi family. They would protect his secret. It was safe for him to continue living as a white man.

Later, his son, Edward Earl, was told the truth by his father. Edward Earl didn't know he had known

~

his real grandmother all his life, since she was a nanny for the Hoovers. Even though he loved her when he was a little boy, he was surprised at first and didn't want to believe it. In his heart, discovering that he had a drop of colored blood hurt him badly, since he was raised to be a white man.

"I'm not going to change now after twenty years as a white man, I don't want to learn how to be a colored man! What do you think will happen to my career with the government in Washington, D.C., if this gets out?" he said to his father.

He was right, of course. In those times the "one drop" rule was how it worked. One drop of colored blood meant you were classified as colored, and colored people weren't appointed to high positions. Period.

Edward Earl's father, Edward Leon, trusted and loved his brothers, but Edward Earl never did care for his uncles in Mississippi. By the time he was fifty years old, he wanted to make a few changes. He didn't trust the Allen's, and he wasn't sure his great-grandfather's master plan would protect him adequately.

"Nobody's threatening you," his father said.

But nothing could change the fact that he saw colored people still oppressed. He knew exactly what would happen to a mulatto man who was passing for white. He thought, *The man would lose everything, and possibly his life.*

No one wanted to hurt him, but Edward Earl believed that the secret gave the Allens the power to control his family if they chose to. Edward Earl figured it was time to separate the lives of his family from the Allens because he thought problems might flare up in the future. After all this I found myself in deep thought about the way the Hoovers in Washington DC, felt later in life.

Remembering, I realized that what my Big Daddy had told me was true. Edward Earl, his wife Carol Lynn, and their son J.E. never visited the Allens again after the 1895 gala.

Edward Earl and his family wanted to move into politics and into higher positions in Washington, D.C. They realized that if the family was caught socializing with niggers, this chance would be gone. Worse, he didn't want anyone to blackmail him with a story about him having colored bloodline. He had to think of a way to separate the Allens from the Hoovers, for good.

Well, he realized that he could blackmail them into keeping their mouths shut. First, he had to tell his wife a lie, so that neither she nor any of their children would know the secret. This is the lie that he told his wife:

"The Allens took my inheritance, the Hoover family ranch in Mississippi," he said.

Carol Lynn was shocked, but what he said next really angered her.

"As if that wasn't enough, now they are trying to say that I have colored blood in my veins!"

"Don't make up details, tell only what you need," was what Master Hoover had told Miss Lilly many years ago. Well, Edward Earl must have inherited some of

262 · *Millie L. McGhee*

his thinking from the Master of Deceit, because in a roundabout way, he actually told his wife the truth, and it certainly worked.

They both cut the Allen's right out of their lives, but that wasn't enough for Edward Earl. He knew he had to work out a master plan to get rid of the Allens forever. He settled on the idea of making a contract with them. Without anyone else knowing, he contacted Clarence Allen.

"If you don't sign this, your whole family could be killed, one by one," he said, then continued, "And Mr. Allen, you got my word on that." The contract stated:

1. The Allens will keep complete silence about the colored blood that runs through the veins of any Hoover. Sign this contract and all the inheritance of the Hoover Plantation will be given to the Allens, cutting out the Hoovers.

2. The Allens in the future can only contact the Hoovers for business, never as relatives.

3. Any Allen upon request can use the Hoover influence in Washington, D.C., to enhance the careers of any member of the Allen family, as long as this contract is kept in order.

"But all of the requests must be within our power, and in exchange for our help with your careers, we require complete silence about our family ties. And mind you, the Secret must be kept forever. If any member of the Allens violates the contract by divulging the family secret, we'll do whatever it takes to protect ourselves."

Signed: "Edward Earl Hoover."

He elaborated on the rules to make sure they were crystal clear. "Now we enter into this agreement knowing all the rules."

The Hoovers would use their power to rid themselves of anyone that threatened them.

By signing this contract, the Hoovers thought they would be free from the Allens forever. They gave all rights to the Hoover Ranch Plantation to the Allens. Years later J.E reinforced the contract by saying, "This is not just for my family, it's for all of us, the Allens and the Hoovers. We must keep father's secrets forever."

This was a political decision made when J.E. Hoover and Clarence Allen II (Big Daddy) grew up and reviewed the contract.

When Emily's seven son, Edward Leon, died, he carried the secret with him. His son, Edward Earl, and grandson, J.E, took over running things. By this time, they knew that J.E.'s career was rising, and they were glad the family secret would not hurt his growing access to power. The Mississippi Hoovers had migrated to Washington, D.C., with the sole exception of Charlotte Hoover, the daughter of the late Joel Edward Hoover, Madam Charlotte's only son. Young Charlotte Hoover moved to Beverly Hills, California, and married a colored man. She

∽

was actually the only pure white Hoover, and she married a colored man. She never contacted the Washington, D.C., Hoovers again, but stayed in contact with the Allens.

In Washington, D.C., Edward Earl had a heart full of anger directed toward his grandparents. He never thought that slaves should have been given equal shares of the ranch. Even though his father was just as colored as any of the Allen brothers, he thought the whole business was just plain wrong.

"Even if it meant giving up the plantation to them, it was worth it. They are out of our lives now," he said to his wife.

J.E. Hoover made up a new story when he grew up, just in case he needed it. He told everyone that Emily Allen was Master Hoover's sister, who died in the 1800s. This was another lie. I found J.E. Hoover to be even more deceitful than the old man Hoover.

J.E. Hoover entered law school, and while he was in law school, he had trouble trying to fit in with the girls, because the colored blood in his veins haunted him. He was afraid to fall in love, because of what would happen if he produced a dark-skinned child. Being colored meant that something was wrong with you in the brain. That's what his mother taught him. Both parents taught him to hate colored people.

Colored People are unintelligent, he told himself.

When he was in grade school, he learned a lot about genes, and how they affect the way children look and act. He also learned that a child could be born with features of ancestors. Genes could reach back many generations. If he ever got married, he knew the family secret might get out, and that was something he didn't want to happen, so he decided to enforce the contract to protect the secret forever. He didn't trust the Allens.

When J.E. thought about his life filled with secrets that came from the body of a slave girl, it always made him unhappy. He found himself hating all colored people, because they reminded him of something he could not accept. He could not even look at one. It became hard for him to talk to a colored person without feeling anger. He found himself with that disease I call, *"Psychosis of Racism."* He hated himself.

Later, when people started to ask why he never married, he started a rumor that he was gay, just because he didn't want to become a father, something he came to fear, knowing that the child's looks might tell the family secret. If he wanted to be with a woman it would be in secret, and the Hoovers had practiced keeping secrets for at least five generations.

When J.E. graduated, he took a job as a clerk in the Justice Department. After receiving his degree in law, he very quickly became the assistant to the Attorney General. He used this position to help Emily's sons get better jobs in the government as white men. This was his way of blackmailing the Allens into keeping his great-grandfather's secret, but he

∾

didn't know that Emily, and all her kin, believed in keeping secrets when they were asked to. He was never in any danger of being exposed by them.

I felt badly for little J.E., taught to hate by his own parents. As a child, he wanted to love his cousins. Through his eyes at that time, he saw no difference.

His mother, Aunt Carol, was another matter; she'd already learned to hate when she was a child. She was very prejudiced. I watched Aunt Carol and I thought she was a very unhappy person. She had so much hate in her heart, it made her look ugly.

This explains why J.E. grew up with so much hate in his heart toward colored people. They told J.E. as he was growing up that the Allens were colored slaves owned by the Hoovers, and that Master Hoover committed a sin by having children with Emily Allen, a colored slave. His father Edward Earl told him the Allens stole his inheritance.

His answer to the race question showed that he felt pretty confused. I decided that I had learned a lot about my roots, and was ready to go home to share this with my family and publish my story in a book for the world to see how hatred kills the human race.

EPILOGUE

When Mrs. Nordstrom found her way back from the past to her husband and children, she was excited and couldn't wait to share all of her excitement. She said breathlessly, "I have so much to tell you all. This was the most exciting experience that I have ever had in my life. Meeting and living among my ancestors was freeing and educational all at the same time. Although I knew this was before my time in life, it was fulfilling, exciting, and beautiful. I found myself wanting to stay with them forever, but I came back because of you, my family. My spirit is free now, and my soul is in acceptance of moving us forward."

When she finally settled down and looked into the eyes of her family, they listened to her every word with joy on their faces. She could tell that they wanted her to share more of her feelings with them, so she shared a poem that she wrote for her people who were labeled, Mulatto.

> When I was a child
> my thoughts were sweet,
> honest, and innocent.
> My mother was white

as a child I saw light-colored skin just like mine.
My father was black, so said the world,
as a child I saw light-colored skin just like mine,
until the world stepped in
I saw no difference.
Through the eyes of a child
people are like a bouquet of flowers,
until the world steps in;
hatred is not born in us,
it's taught.
That is my philosophy.

"That was a great poem my dear, and you are right! Our society makes us feel and think different with all of its different standards," said her husband.

They all gave her a hug, and the children were ready for more, they were enjoying the storytelling.

"Mother, tell us about how you felt growing up labeled a 'Mulatto,'" one of the children asked.

"I will tell you all about my life in another book some-day. I am tired now and need some sleep," she said.

The children were sad, but understood.

"Maybe tomorrow she will tell us the story as she writes it in a new book," replied Mr. Nordstrom.

After many years of sleepless nights, Mr. and Mrs. Nordstrom were ready for many years of happiness and hope for sleep with peaceful dreams and won-derful thoughts. She was so happy about learning so much about her ancestor, as well as forgiveness to those who worked with notorious and racist policies. She felt her work sheds new light on the fact that keeping secrets does more harm than good, and reminds people that we are all each a vital part of the same human family.

She decided to work on her next book about what she believes will help her children understand the secrets she herself has kept in her own life.

"Yes, children the next book will be written soon, and you too will understand more about my past and future," said Mrs. Nordstrom.

This was the first night in a long time that Mr. and Mrs. Nordstrom slept like babies with sweet dreams with a great future ahead.

For more information on the intriguing
history between Hoovers and the Allens, visit:
http://www.whatsdoneinthedarkmovie.com/